Celebrating Men

By

B. Niles

Published by B. Niles Books
Book cover design by Eugene Miti of Globalten
Edited by Sandra Hicks of Solid Journey

Library of Congress Cataloging in Publication Data

Niles, B.
CELEBRATING MEN.

1. Family & Relationships
2. Spiritual life

ISBN 1-45-385790-7

Dedicated to:
My wonderful mom, Joan Elaine Niles,
who sacrificed herself continuously for her family and for her Lord.

"Her children arise and call her blessed…
Give her the reward she has earned,
And let her works bring her praise at the city gate."
- Proverbs 31: 38-31

Contents

Acknowledgments

This project was inspired by God and developed with the aid of so many people he put in my life to encourage and assist me with its completion. Therefore, I want to thank the Lord first and foremost for his grace, mercy and love. He pushed me and prodded me to get this book done and guided me to the right people to make sure it came to pass. So to God be all the glory and honor.

Next I would like to thank my mom, Joan Niles, always my number one supporter in all that I undertake. She believes in me second only to Christ. Thanks mom for your faithful prayers, encouragement and support.

There were also a number of people that aligned themselves with God and me in his plan for *Celebrating Men.* John Leconte, one of my best friends, told me to put my thoughts and experiences into a book. Well, John, here it is! Thank you for always being there for me. Travis Allen and Anita Boulware, some of the best friends a girl could have, thank you for always being my staunch supporters. Anita, you told me years ago, "Beverly, you have a ministry to men." I don't even know if you remember telling me that and I don't know why you said it, but as it turns out, you may be right. Mihret Amare, my daughter, yes you're also a friend, but I'll always think of you and call you my daughter. You remind me so much of me. Thank you for always believing and dreaming with me.

Then there were those who took the time out of their busy schedules to review the book in its early stages and gave me their feedback. You just don't know how valuable your input was to me and I want to thank you so much for your generosity and encouragement to continue. These special people were: LaVerne

Niles, Mihret Amare, the Honorable Judge Bob Davis, Pastor Sullivan McGraw and Tenell Rhodes, Sr. Look what you've helped bring to pass. I hope you're pleased with the outcome. Thank you for partnering with me in bringing this to fruition.

Finally, thank you to Eugene Miti of Globalten for the cover and website designs, Editor, Sandra Hicks of Solid Journey, and the number of people who pre-purchased copies of this book before it was even published because of their belief in me. There are too many of you to mention all by name here, but you were also an integral part of bringing project, *Celebrating Men* into reality.

Thank you all and my prayer is that the Lord will bless you abundantly for your service to him and me. You've blessed me richly.

Foreword

Have you ever spoken with someone and immediately been inspired by their presence and conversation? Have you ever had someone tell you a story or testimony that just seemed simply unbelievable, especially given the context of today's increasingly depraved society and wayward moral compass? *Celebrating Men* is a surprisingly refreshing and hearty, yet easily digested look into how things should be despite how they are regarding men in the modern world. It is a young and vibrant Christian woman's journey through life with men and her take on how the many experiences affected and influenced her, and how they could and should have been improved based on practical godly principles. This is neither a male-bashing nor men-worshipping work, but rather, a rare opportunity for men (and those who love them) to take a look through the view of a woman at the intended purpose and impact men can and should have on the girls and women of all ages in their lives.

Most men and women reading this will likely find some common thoughts or experiences and will find themselves doing both an inward evaluation and that of the other person's reactions to determine how they could have handled matters differently. This is not your garden-variety self-help journal or male empowerment instructional guide. This book will make those genuinely seeking to be all God intended them to be consider that real Christianity is lived faithfully one moment, interaction and relationship at a time. It will challenge, inspire and cause self-examination of motives, methods, and mindsets.

Though there are many publications a person may encounter, prepare to have your perspective on men and their God-given role shaken, stirred and perhaps permanently shifted in order to better recognize yourself and your own role as man or woman. This is highly recommended reading material for men. In addition, though I cannot speak authoritatively from a woman's perspective, I can say that women would also greatly benefit from reading these pages because, as they'll discover, if you expect more, you'll get more and you must inspect what you expect.

Tenell Rhodes, Sr.
Senior Vice President
General Digital Corporation

Introduction

The symbol of the clay jar on this book carries with it an interesting story and gives a type of summary of the message of the book. The graphic artist I worked with had not read the book but wanted to know more about it in order to produce an applicable cover. I believe the title of the book may have inspired him along with my inscription on the back cover. So when he produced the first draft of the front cover instead of the jar you now see, there was a beautiful crown. The cover looked great, but I couldn't help chuckling. The crown didn't quite sit right with me for a few reasons. Though I agreed with the message of the crown that the man is the head and king of his household, I thought the crown too bold and premature. I showed it to a female friend and she got very annoyed. I laughed outright this time at her knee-jerk reaction. So we tried the crown of thorns since the King of Kings gave up his royal crown for one of thorns. I thought it might be a good message. When I showed the same friend and asked what she thought, her first response was that it brought to mind suffering. I rejected that crown too, because that wasn't what the book conveyed.

The next morning as I awoke and spent some time with the Lord, the enlightened clay jar symbol came to mind. I was led to 2 Corinthians 4:6 which reads that God "…made his light shine in our hearts to give us the light of the knowledge of the glory of God in the face of Christ." The passage further, in verse 7, says that "...we have this treasure in jars of clay to show that this all-surpassing power is from God and not from us." That was it! That symbol embodied the message of this book. God put his treasure in jars of clay–men, to show forth his surpassing power. The clay represents common, from the earth, but moldable, pliable in the master potter's hands. It's the light of God, the deposit of the Holy Spirit that makes the jars so beautiful and valuable. We hold the treasure of God within us. Now how that is manifested in each life and throughout different stages of life is what this book touches on.

Clay has different states of being, depending on its environment. It can be fine-grained soil that's "plastic" like when moist, or hard when fired. Clay takes on innumerable forms when fired. God has created clay jars to house the treasure of himself. So how does this relate to celebrating men? Regardless of the state the man is currently in, like clay, if he becomes like putty in God's hands, he can become something incredibly beautiful. In fact, man, because he is created in the image of God is already a wonder, but when pliable in the Master's hands, he becomes a work of art and honor.

In summary, I'd say this book is about belief and faith in men and in God working through some men and in spite of others. If we truly believe the Word of God that says that "...all things God works for the good of those who love him, who have been called according to his purpose" (Romans 8:28). Then that also applies to the men and therefore the stigma that many women have against men should be eradicated.

Much of the background for this book reads as a one-sided autobiography. I draw from my relationships with men and the role they played in shaping my life. I want to celebrate and show honest appreciation for the men in my life, to depict an overall gratefulness to God for men and the role they play in our lives and to hopefully show an example of God's sovereignty, love and faithfulness in working all things together for good, regardless of some painful experiences.

I am not a scholar. I have not achieved any great accomplishments or honors. I am not a great athlete or famed individual sharing my memoirs. I am simply a young woman that has a remarkable testimony of how God used men to shape who I am today—a lovely, 45 year old virgin.

I choose to see reasons to be thankful for the men God brought into my life and helped to fashion who I am today, whether the experiences felt good at the time or whether they were quite painful. I appreciate and enjoy our intrinsic differences. I find it fascinating. It would have been too easy to allow a few painful experiences to cloud my appreciation of a good thing, meaning men. If I had, I would have missed out on some wonderful friendships and experiences.

Didn't God say to give thanks in all things? Not only did he say give thanks in all things, but he took it even further and said, "Rejoice in the Lord always." He emphasized it by saying, "I will say it again: Rejoice!" Rejoicing over something is even more potent than to just be thankful. So I had to take it up a notch. I'm not just thankful for men, I celebrate them!

John, who is one of my best friends, encouraged me to write this book. As a result of conversations we'd had over the years about our different relationships and friendships, one day John said, "Beverly, you need to write a book." At first I began to write about living single as a Christian woman or man. Part one of the book was about how God kept me and part two about how to live single and honor God in our relationships. I stopped working on the book for about four years and when I finally picked it up again to complete the project, I felt as though part one needed to stand alone.

What was so ironic about the writing of this book to celebrate men, both the men that were instrumental in molding my life and those like them, is that I was a 30 something year old virgin (now 45 year old virgin), writing a book about men! My ex-fiancé, said, "What could you possibly have to write about men when you have no experience?" What he meant, I think, is that since I had no sexual experience, had never been married, nor lived with a man outside of my brothers, what experience could I have? (By the way men, does everything have to revolve around sex? I mean I know it's said to be the number one desire for you, but is it the be all and end all of getting to know a man? There is more to you, right? That's what I thought.) So my answer to the cynic is, "I have the best kind of experience that is not clouded by painful, cynical emotions from a broken, jilted heart." That's not to say that I haven't been hurt, jilted or skeptical of men–I can attest to all of the above. It's just that God has kept me. He kept my mind, body, soul and spirit in the midst of it all so that I would not become unforgiving, broken and jaded, but rather, I became full of expectancy and promise; full of his grace, full of his love, peace and mercy. So when I reflected on my life, I saw him using primarily men to teach me various lessons and truths about God's grace, love and about relationships.

A friend of mine asked, "What about your mom and the women in your life; didn't you learn from them?" Of course I did, my mom being the female that made the most impact. However, for whatever the reason and because of how I am wired, God used the men most to teach, inspire and mold me.

I am excited about this book and pray that it will encourage you, if you're a man, to live up to your God-given potential. If you're a woman reading this, soften your heart, renew your mind and gain wisdom on how to guard your heart and encourage the men in your life to be all they can be. I marvel at God's beauty and greatness as I think of how good he's been to me and of the way he's used men to show me that I'm a lovely, intelligent, appealing woman, and desirable mate. My hat's off to these men.

The men that I'm celebrating are those who take responsibility for their actions even at great risk and sacrifice; men who are not afraid to stand up for what is right and aren't afraid to lead; men who don't allow their wives to run roughshod over them but recognize their God-given role as the head of their household; men who parent their children; men of honor who are loyal to their word to be faithful to their wives; men who provide for their families and serve as examples in their churches, and communities; men who respect women, as God intended- as their equal in value, if not in position; men who are not given to excuses as to why they can't, but commit to finding ways to get the job done, whatever the task may be; and finally, to those men who appreciate and desire the differences and assets of a woman and do not seek a mate of his own sex. Men who recognize that woman was created for man, not man created for man. These men I've described are the rock and backbone of our communities and make us and our nation strong. This is not to say that they have not fallen. Most of us aren't batting a thousand in every area of our lives every day. Please don't misunderstand. They're not perfect; they simply own up, stand up and fight to get better.

To those of you who are driven to protect, lead and serve God, your family and your community… Thank you! I celebrate you.

Chapter One

First Impression of Manhood

"First impressions are constant in society…
Good ones are pleasant and long lasting,
Bad ones long and difficult to disprove."
~ Diego Velasquez

"Train a child in the way he should go,
and when he is old he will not turn from it."
~ Proverbs 22:6

First Impression of Manhood

Dad was my first example of manly parenting, of what a husband was like, of how men treat women and of how men interact with other men. He gave me value as a child, he was my protector; he was even my first example of what God might be like, even though my dad did not profess to be God-fearing.

My dad and my mom were both instrumental in forming my first impression of manhood. Though I will focus primarily on my dad's involvement in molding my image of men, I would be remiss if I didn't also share my mom's involvement in molding my image of men as well. My parents separated when I was just eight years old. During my childhood and teen years, my mom never spoke ill of my father. He deserted the family both in presence and support, but Mom never openly showed any derision of him in front of us. It wasn't until I was an adult that Mom told me her side of the story behind the separation and even then, it was only in response to some accusations I made to her about marrying a man who showed signs that he wouldn't be faithful from the very beginning.

When my father did come to visit us, Mom was always loving and respectful and made sure we were respectful as well. Her treatment of him in both word and deed during those years spoke volumes to me about my mom, her faith, fatherhood and respect for the role of husbands.

In our eyes, Dad may not have deserved our respect because of his actions and Mom was not ignorant of his faults. The Word of God, however, says for wives to be submissive to your husbands. Some translations say obey or respect, and for children to "Honor your father and mother…" If these passages are read within their full context, they're not just referring to when the husband or parents are good or wonderful, but because

God commanded it to be so. It's easy to obey and honor when a husband is wonderful or parents are great, anyone can love and do the right thing under those conditions. It is more difficult, however, to do so when they are self-seeking, harsh or absent. The command to honor them still stands.

"It's easy to obey and honor when a husband is wonderful or parents are great, anyone can love and do the right thing under those conditions. It is more difficult however, to do so when they are self-seeking, harsh or absent. The command to honor them still stands."

Fathers, you have an awesome responsibility and opportunity. You have the opportunity to impact lives, communities and even countries through your influence beginning right in your own homes. Think of the great men in history and great men of today that have impacted your lives. Most of them were someone's father or someone's son.

My dad was an absent parent most of my life, but whether present or absent, he still made an impact. We have heard that both verbal and non-verbal language can be powerful and effective. I believe a similar principle holds true also for the impact of a parent that is present and active in their child's life as well as a parent that is absent and inactive in their child's life.

I am grateful for the few memories of times shared with Dad and the lessons that came about as a result of those times. One of the things Dad taught me to do is to use my mind. He used board games to teach us to think and reason. He almost always walked with a board game when he came to visit. He liked to communicate, challenge and compete. Dad taught me to live and enjoy life by his example. Be free, no matter what others think about you. (Though he was not the most moral of men, the message sent was, live, enjoy and be free. My mom taught me the godly version.) Finally, Dad taught me a lesson of great impact on my life, he made me see that I am a princess. I don't recall him ever calling me a princess; he just always made me feel like one. That instilled such confidence in me at a young age. It didn't really matter ultimately what anyone else said, I felt that, to my dad, I was a princess, I was beautiful and special.

My dad was born in 1934 on the island of Trinidad and Tobago to strict God-fearing parents who had little money. He is dark in complexion, six feet tall, intelligent with a wry sense of humor, and he was quite handsome in his younger years. He was the second child born to his parents and he had six siblings. Dad didn't speak very fondly of his childhood, however. In fact, he spoke of his childhood with bitterness and even anger. The most vivid memories I recall him sharing with me were of his father tying him to a tree and beating him for something he either had done or failed to do (I no longer remember which) and of the early morning chores his dad made him do for the neighbors as an act of brotherly love, before he could do his own chores for the family. His family didn't have running water, so he had to go down the street to a water pump and get buckets of water for the family to cook, clean and bathe. He resented the strictness of his dad and the poverty he grew up in.

It seemed to me, though he never said this directly to me, that Dad decided he wasn't ever going to be poor in his adult life and that he was going to enjoy life because he didn't see his parents enjoy life. This would make sense to me based on what I observed of his life.

Dad married my mom, a very strong woman of faith in Christ, but he himself, though well versed in scripture from being raised in the church, didn't have a personal relationship with Christ. At least that is the impression I got from him as I grew up. He and my mom had five children, but their relationship was rocky and fraught with physical violence that left physical and emotional scars on them both.

Dad has a total of eight children. If you were to interview each of his children, I'm certain each would give you a different picture of him and what he means to each of them. But without a doubt he's made an indelible mark and influence on the life of each one. In some cases, he is viewed with resentment, in some with indifference, in some he's viewed with sadness and regret, some with fondness and I hope with love. I can't speak for the others, only for myself.

Dad had many faults. There was a lot he probably did wrong. I blamed him a lot. There's so much that he missed by not being involved in our lives. I was angry with him for most of my teen and early adult years because he wasn't there for me. I was angry with him for not being there to protect me and teach me about men. It's sad that he didn't watch me bud into womanhood, wasn't at any of my graduations, never saw me dance, only met one of my boyfriends, never bought me a dress, that I know of. But God knew and God fathered me where my father failed.

In spite of all that Dad failed to do, I still remember special moments. I must have been about five or six years old when he had me to dance for some visitors at our home in New York. Dad liked to hobnob with the wealthy and tried to expose us to that life. When we stayed with him, we went on his friends' yachts, stayed in beach homes, and visited his wealthy, well educated friends and business owners. But two of the most meaningful memories for me were the insight Dad gave me on a particular occasion in reference to a male friend and when he gave me his personal pinky ring to always remember him. These two things sound so simple, so small, but sometimes it's those small things that may seem insignificant, that make a world of difference. What were some of the things that impacted your life? What were some of your fondest memories growing up? I bet some of the most memorable were not the big fanfare moments, but some of the small things or moments shared with your dad or loved one.

When I was 30 years old I met a man that I found attractive but his communication confused me. You see, though I was 30, I wasn't very worldly or experienced and as my younger sister would say, I was naïve in regards to men. The guy was a little older than I, well-built, very attractive, loved the Lord and of great character. When we met, however, I'd made it clear I was only open to friendship. I had been engaged not long before and even though the engagement was broken, I strongly believed that my ex-fiancé was the man for me. I just believed it wasn't our time yet. Therefore, this new friend would be wasting his time if he sought more than friendship from me. He said he understood and would respect my stand but he continued to address me with endearments that I thought were more appropriate for romantic relationships. Every now and then I had to remind him about what I told him in the beginning. He said the endearments didn't mean anything; it was just how he expressed himself in general. I perceived it might be a southern thing. In my culture it meant something and his expression made me uncomfortable.

Around the time this new friendship was developing, Dad came for a visit. During the visit, I shared the situation with Dad and asked his opinion. He told me, "Don't believe that your friend does not mean anything by his endearments. He obviously likes you, wants to be with you, wants more than a friendship but is trying to respect your stand because you don't want a relationship." Dad put my mind at ease. It meant so much to me to be able to talk with him about it. I wish I could have shared stuff like that with him all my life. It was the only time I ever shared anything personal with Dad.

Today I'm ever observant of fathers with their sons and daughters. I watch them with joy, a little envy and even wonderment. I don't really know what it's like to have a father in my life, to have a father there for me, so I learn through watching the interaction of other families. I watch in wonderment because one, it looks so good, but then, I also find it so hard to believe. You know, are they real? Are there really men who truly care about their children? Or are they all hard, uncaring and uncommunicative? I know that can't be true because I see several examples of loving fathers both in my brothers who are incredibly responsible and caring fathers and also at church and through a few friendships. One thing I admire at our church is that there are so many men, both married men of all ages with children and single young adult men and teenage boys. Our Pastor, Sullivan McGraw, is a great example as a husband and father. He also has a dynamic ministry to men of all ages. We need more mentors, mentors who first model by example then take responsibility to teach the younger men about what it means to be a godly man.

Fathers, I couldn't stress to you how important you are in the lives of your children and how unique your role is in their lives. You have so much power and influence in the minds and lives you shape through your children. Some of you reading this right now may not be biological fathers, but you are raising children as stepfathers, teachers, mentors, coaches, and more. Realize that, though many times your investment may seem insignificant or unappreciated, the impact or return on your investment, long and short term, is great. Remember the male role models in your life, whether they were positive or negative, whether it was due to their presence or absence. They influenced your life and your outlook and you are having a similar impact or influence on the children in your life today. Fathers, you are your sons and daughters first impression of manhood. You also give your daughter her first impression of the value of womanhood by how you treat your wife, your mother and your sisters.

Though my father was the first example of manhood in my life, there were a few others that made early, lasting impressions as well. At the age of 11, my siblings and I were sent back home to the West Indies to live with a family that was not related to us. The couple had three big, strong, very masculine sons (that's how they appeared to my 11 year old eyes). The two elder sons were about six feet tall and the youngest one about 5 feet 10 inches. They were not slender or obese. They did a lot of physical labor and were very athletic and muscular. The two younger sons roughed us up a lot. They also chose to sexually molest me and one of my younger sisters (at different times and unknown to each other, I think). I was the oldest of my siblings sent to live with the family and at age 12, I was very feminine and shapely. The eldest of the two culprits chose not only to harass us kids during the day (he seemed to take pleasure in "beating the tar out of us" with a belt whenever he felt we did something wrong), but he also sexually harassed me at night. He would come into our bedroom late at night when we were asleep and fondle my breasts, touch my private parts and on occasion he attempted to penetrate me. I don't remember anything else, just what was most uncomfortable or what hurt the most. I don't even remember how long this occurred or how many times. What remain are only the discomfort, pain and relief of how it all came to an end.

As I reflect on this experience, I see the Lord was looking out for my siblings and me. You see, it was a blessing that the family took us in but they now had four extra mouths to feed. Let me rewind. When my mom and dad separated years before, Mom had five children to support on her own. She often worked 2-3 jobs. My elder brother, who was six years older than I, was given the responsibility to care for us when Mom went to work. He disliked the responsibility and as a result, he abused it. At one point I tried to run away. At this time in our lives we were living in the United States in an urban city, in a low income, crime infested part of the city. We were constantly in fights and Mom feared for our future. She thought it best to send the four youngest of us back to our country for a few years to allow us to experience the culture, live in a Christian environment (the family we stayed with were Christians), in a place with little crime, and in an environment that would allow us freedom and more time to simply be children.

Now the blessing I'm speaking of in this situation is that my three siblings and I slept in one room and all in the same bed. It was a blessing for two reasons. One reason is because if either of the sons tried anything too severe or energetic while we slept it would have caused a stir which would have awakened everyone. (His younger brother was also sexually molesting my younger sister at different times. I don't know if they were each aware of what the other was doing.) I always slept on the end of the bed and my brother one year younger than I, slept on the other end. We slept in alternated head to foot positions, i.e., if I slept with my head to the headboard, my sister slept next to me with her head to the footboard, my other sister with her head to the headboard and my brother with his head to the footboard. The second reason for thanksgiving is that one night my brother was awakened and later saved us by telling the father of these young adults (they were 18 and 19 years old). God was looking out for us but the experience still embittered me. It created distrust, anger and maybe even hatred in me and it was years before I realized the impact and obtained healing.

My first impression of men was mixed. By the time I was 12 years old, the examples I'd seen were that of selfishness. I love my dad but he deserted his parental responsibilities in pursuit of fortune and pleasures. The young men in whose home we stayed fed their sexual pleasure at the expense of my sister and me. The picture of men that was developing before me was not attractive, but God is faithful and did not leave me to flounder. Possibly the brightest segment of the picture during those early years was of Uncle Dan, the young men's father. He was a spot of gold. He was gruff most of the time, but caring, strong and godly. Uncle Dan took us in because he cared. He had four children of his own he'd already raised. He did not have to take in four more children. His example and influence tempered the distrust and cynicism towards men that was forming in my mind. I thank God for Uncle Dan and for men like him. I wish there were more.

First Impression
Application

1) Whether your father was present and involved in your life or not, what was your first impression of him? Describe him.

____

____

2) How do you feel about your dad? Do you want to be like him?

____

____

3) Who are some of the other men or women in your life that have impacted your life and why?

____

____

4) Whose lives have you impacted or influenced for good or bad? ____

____

5) How does it make you feel to know that you are making an impact on future generations and that your positive or negative influence will be remembered and possibly continued?

____

____

____

Chapter Two

Innocent Trials

"My brethren, count it all joy
when you fall into various trials,
knowing that the testing of your faith produces patience."
~ James 1:2, 3 (NKJV)

Innocent Trials

The second "man" in my life was but a child at the time, he was 11 years old and a relative. I was nine years old. Our families lived near each other. One night I woke up in the middle of the night to find my cousin over me and sticking his tongue unceremoniously down my throat. I woke up, fought him off and promptly vomited. That was my introduction to kissing and I found it absolutely repulsive. That experience made me never want to kiss another human being in my life. (Thankfully, my opinion on that activity changed in my later years.) But I mention this because it did affect my thinking at an early age, which also affected my actions. If it had been a positive experience, I might have been tempted to welcome such advances or even seek such opportunities too early in life. I thank God now when I reflect on the experience and that it was a negative experience. It probably helped to keep me innocent for a long time.

I can also see in a similar light, the two young men that I mentioned in the first chapter that sexually molested my sister and me when we were children. I don't believe they were being malicious or seeking to harm us. They were 18 and 19 years old, Christian young men that were feeling their oats, so to speak. They wanted to explore sexually but knew they should not fornicate. They also probably didn't have much opportunity with the way the culture was back in the 70's in Trinidad in a Christian home. I also think that my sister and I living there in their home presented them with the temptation and the opportunity to explore. They were, however, old enough to know better and to know the ramification their actions would have on us as children. It was selfish on their part. It really wasn't "innocent" trials in their case. After all, they weren't 12 or 13 year olds playing a game of house.

As horrible an experience as this was to my sister and me, I can now still see some good. God kept the brother that was attempting to use me sexually from penetrating me. The Lord also used my brother to save us before things got more severe. My 11 year old brother went and told their dad what he saw one evening. Their dad immediately took action and dealt with them and they never touched us like that again. Uncle Dan was a hard yet loving father to them and us. I'm so grateful, once again, for God's protection and provision through this man. It could have turned out much differently. What if Uncle Dan had ignored my brother's report or disregarded his sons' activity as normal behavior that they would outgrow? What if he hadn't cared enough about us to do anything? The story could have had a much worse ending.

I describe "innocent trials" as sexually explorative activity among children and youths. From childhood through early teen years we are curious and explorative. We like to play house and doctor/patient games because we want to explore what it's all about, explore our bodies and relationships, and imitate the adult examples we see. Television and other forms of media in general, have opened the world up to us, both the good and the bad. It's natural for us to have questions and want to try things out if we've been exposed to them. If our parents aren't talking to us about such issues as sex, sexuality, drugs, and pornography, then we can learn about them inappropriately and try to explore these mysterious territories inappropriately. If parents are paying attention and involved in their children's lives, they would know their children better than any teacher. Learning about sex, sexuality and sensuality should be taught first by parents considering the society we live in today. Many parents, however, may not even know themselves and feel incompetent or intimidated by the task of teaching their children about these areas of life.

I wonder how many men talk with their sons about their sexual desires, about what to expect early on and throughout their teen years and adulthood. I wonder how many fathers actually sit down with their daughters and converse with them about what to expect from boys, what boys look for, and how to avoid certain traps? I wonder how many mothers talk to their daughters about the changes their bodies, their hormones and their emotions will go through and how to handle the changes? I dare say we aren't talking about it enough with our children and many of them have to find out by experimentation first and this can often leave scars for life–scars that were preventable.

> "I dare say we aren't talking about it [sex and sexuality] enough with our children and many of them have to find out by experimentation first and this can often leave scars for life; scars that were preventable."

On at least three occasions, before I was 15, I had close relatives that were younger than I fondle me or try to kiss me while they thought I was sleeping (two were male and one was female). Since they were children, I believe it was more out of curiosity than malicious intent. I was not an angel myself. I can recall a couple of incidents, before age 15, when I too tried a couple experiments of my own. How much of this was prompted by hormones and how much by environmental awareness, I don't know. But it's happened enough in my personal scope and I have heard enough from friends and family members, as well as seen enough on television to know that it's an issue that should be addressed more consistently and in the right settings such as with parents, youth groups, churches and lastly, schools. The schools should aid the parents to do the education more than take the role of parents in teaching about sexuality and morals. Empower the parents so they can educate their children on these sensitive, moral issues. I think parents would do more if they felt better equipped to do so. Raise parental awareness of the need to address these subjects with their children early on (depending on the individual development of the children), rather than after the children have already started experimenting.

I know of two nationally broadcast radio programs that rigorously seek to empower parents to teach their children about some of these issues: "Family Talk," hosted by Dr. James Dobson and "Family Life Today," hosted by Dennis Rainey and Bob Lepine. I'm sure there are others that I don't know about, but I certainly don't think that it's being taught anywhere near the scale that it should be taught when you consider how children are inundated with a daily supply of immoral messages from television programming, their peers, billboards, magazines at the check-out stands etc. I am neither a psychologist, doctor, counselor nor expert on child or adult psychology. I'm simply speaking from personal experience and from having worked with teenagers and children for 26 years.

Fathers, I encourage you to be alert and cautious of the people that you have around your children. Be watchful of the men and women or boys and girls that you allow to babysit, mentor or befriend your children. Don't be paranoid, but be observant and prayerful who you allow to engage your children. Get to know the families of the friends of your children. Go to their schools and meet their teachers and coaches. Participate in their lives and let would-be predators know that you're involved in your children's lives. Talk to your children. Keep the lines of communication open; educate them about sex and sexuality. Educate them about sexual desires, lust and behaviors to be conscious of and how to deal with them. Seventeen years ago I started researching and teaching on abstinence and using the "Why Wait" materials from Josh McDowell (which are unfortunately not available anymore). Recent reports show that "73% of sexual assaults are perpetrated by *non-strangers.* Two out of three rapes are committed by someone known to the victim!" (RAINN-Rape, Abuse and Incest National Network) "Four out of ten girls who first had intercourse at 13 or 14 reported it was either non-voluntary or unwanted." ("Facts and Stats" National Campaign Key Statistics).

It's so sad to me that men who were created to be protectors have instead become perpetrators, and predators who prey on the weak and helpless. That's why I applaud those men who stand up for what is right, stand their ground and live up to their God-given roles as protectors of their families and of the weaker vessels in their communities. James 1:27 gives a good indication of what's important to the heart of God. He says that, "Religion that God our Father accepts as pure and faultless is this: to look after orphans and widows in their distress and to keep oneself from being polluted by the world."

Satan is as a roaring lion seeking whom he may devour. He picks off the weak and vulnerable ones first. You father, you husband, you big brother, you teacher, you coach, you neighbor, are a covering for our children, our widows and our single women. The African saying that it takes a village to raise a child needs to be truer today than ever before with the prevalence of evil all around. We need you. As the saying goes, "The only thing it takes for evil to prevail is for good men to do nothing." What are you doing to make a difference?

Innocent Trials

<u>Application</u>

1) What experiences or trials from your childhood have had a major impact on your life?

____

____

2) What kind of impact have they had on your life?

____

____

3) We know that in ALL things God works it out for the good of those who love him. How is God using the circumstances in your life for your good? (For some it may be hard to find the good but search prayerfully.)

____

____

____

Chapter Three

My Super Hero

"…While we were still sinners,
Christ died for us."
~ Romans 5:8

My Super Hero

In puberty, I met Jesus Christ, and welcomed him into my life as my Lord and Savior. Without him I would be lost and certainly not be who I am today. Because I surrendered my life to him at a young age, I allowed the Word of God and the Holy Spirit to mold my thinking and therefore mold me. You see, coupled with the lessons learned from the negative and premature sexual advances I'd experienced, I learned early in my walk with the Lord that sex before marriage was sin and therefore taboo to me. I read a multitude of romances as a teenager, (I read an average of five books a week between the ages of 12 and 15) but back then they were clean and advocated virginity and purity. Those books reinforced the principle of purity in relationships that I was gathering from the scriptures. Purity was also taught and modeled at the church I attended. Despite the negative experiences during those years, there was so much good I was still learning without even realizing it.

Jesus is a true superhero. He rescued me from sin and as I studied his Word and grew in my faith and the application of his Word, I received the best prevention education for all types of evils: premarital sex, drugs, unforgiveness, lying, and hatred, to name a few. His Word and the Holy Spirit taught me true value of self. Hey, he died for me. How special is that?! Batman, Spiderman, Superman, Wonder Woman, Ninja Turtles, the X-men (Okay, so I'm dated, I don't have children to keep up with who the new super heroes are, so what do you expect?) My point is, however, none of them died for me! None of them rose from the dead and even if they did, they're fictional! I could probably also name some real life super heroes like Martin Luther King, Jr., Rosa Parks, Benjamin Franklin, Presidents Nelson Mandela and Barack Obama, just to mention a few. The fact is, however, no matter how great they were or are none of them can compare to Jesus, Son of Man yet Son of God, natural yet supernatural, a real super hero. The others have done wonderful things, but none are deity or have the power of deity. None of them could release us from the bonds of sin and free us from the true slavery that resides within. No one else has the ability to position us in our rightful places as heirs to the kingdom of God most high.

At any rate, I can't say enough about Jesus Christ. I know no man or woman can fully live up to his example because he's the only one who's never sinned. We were born in sin; we have all sinned. However, he has given us his Holy Spirit. We have a deposit of him, a deposit of greatness within. That's pretty incredible when you think about it. He died so that we might live. (Who else would do that for you?) He died so that he could live in all of us through his Holy Spirit. If he still lived in fleshly form he would have been limited to time and space and his leverage and power also curtailed. But God's mastermind plan to send him to earth to be born almost as we were, to live as we do but as with one hand tied behind his back, so to speak, to suppress his power took incredible love and wisdom. Every step he took, every decision he made, he was thinking of us. He gave up his desires, his rights, his crown, and himself for us. I can't help but deeply admire and deeply worship him for that.

It is because of my love and awe of the Lord, that sometimes even when I didn't feel his love and went the way of rebellion, that simple fear and reverence for him kept me and I still chose to obey. When I was ridiculed for my stand for purity (which by the way, I believe is more than just abstinence from sexual intercourse) or when my own flesh screamed for affection and attention, because of what he endured for me, most of the time, I fought to do what would please him. This does not just apply to sexual fulfillment, but to everything, from what I chose to wear, to whether I would retaliate in a disagreement, to the choice of whether to lie about something to make myself look better. WWJT (What would Jesus think?) or WWJF (What would Jesus feel?) or WJBP (Would Jesus be pleased?) Ultimately, his thoughts of me were

> "He's done far more for me than any other and cares for me more than any other, so doesn't it stand to reason that his opinion matters above any other?"

far more important, in most cases, than what my peers thought and still think today. He's done far more for me than any other and cares for me more than any other, so doesn't it stand to reason that his opinion matters above any other?

Therefore, I attribute the life changing influence and the sustaining power of Jesus in the formative years of my life as the primary reason why I choose to celebrate men today. I am fully aware that none of us are perfect. We've all fallen whether man or woman. Men, being the more dominant, prominent, physically stronger sex and leaders by design are therefore the easier to fault, the easier to blame, at least from a female perspective. But because of the love of God and the redemptive work of Christ, I see the beauty in men. I can see what God created man to be because of the revelation of Christ. I look at men with expectation and higher purpose. As God looks at us and sees us through the blood of his Son Jesus with a higher purpose and has higher expectations than we ourselves might have, so too I look at you, man with high expectations and purpose. I've heard it said, "You get what you expect." That may be another one of the reasons why I've had so many good and pure relationships with men, it's what I expect.

In the Old Testament and in the New Testament of the Bible I see examples of God's love, perception and value of man in spite of man's failures and shortcomings. There are two examples, in particular, that speak loudest to me. First there's the example of David. David murdered Uriah in order to get Bathsheba, Uriah's beautiful wife. Yet God still referred to David as a man after God's own heart. David failed. David sinned. David fell short. But his heart wasn't to live in sin. David repented and turned from his sin and wickedness because he loved God. He recognized his sin. He felt grief and remorse over his sin. He confessed his sin and turned from it because David loved God. He wasn't perfect. He killed a man and as a result, the son conceived in his sin also died. His sin affected several generations. (The repercussions of sin can often transcend generations and influence countless lives.) David did wrong, he did evil in the sight of God and man, but God saw his repentant heart and forgave him. God saw his heart and restored him and thereafter, David followed God faithfully.

In the New Testament I think of Saul of Tarsus, later called the apostle Paul, who persecuted the church and had thousands of Christians killed in his zealousness for Jehovah. In reality, he was fighting against the purposes of God in his zealousness but didn't realize it. He was killing the people God sent His only Son to die for. Yet God saved him, turned him around and used him mightily for the kingdom of God. God saw his heart. He was misguided in his persecution, but pure in purpose. He thought the Christian Jews were heretics, a plague to be extinguished rather than allowed to spread and pollute the people of God. He was trying to help God in his own way. I think God saw his heart and set him on the right path. God perceived Paul differently than you and I would have. God had a plan, knew Saul's potential and true, but misguided heart. God stopped him in his tracks, got his attention for three days and nights by blinding him. He was then open to truly listen to God. His heart just needed molding. He was now ready to hear and obey.

If it wasn't for God where would we be? If it wasn't for his redemptive work through Christ which is able to transform the most degenerate of lives, man's current course would be incomprehensibly worse than it is today. I thank God for the example we have in Christ and in the men that strive to be Disciples of Christ. These men who are being conformed into the image of Christ make many mistakes–they fall, but with humility they rise and fight to be heroes to their loved ones and communities.

That's why Jesus, the true transformer, is my super hero. He's done what no one else could ever do. He's completely transformed the lives of countless men, women and children for eternity. He's given life, hope, joy and peace of mind. He's lived the example and encourages man to live up to his God given purpose, and ideal and then empowers him to be able to do so. What a God! What a man!

He's given direction to the lost and purpose to the downcast. He's healed countless people and opened a door that no one else could. He's restored us to our rightful places as children of God. He's given us power to overcome sin and death and given us access to the throne room of God our Father. Who else can do all this? Who else has such power? Who else has such wisdom? Therefore, who else deserves our homage?

Look up! It's a bird, no, it's a plane, no, it's super man, the real one – Christ. (I couldn't resist.)

My Super Hero
<u>Application</u>

1) Who is the hero in your life and why? What has he/she done for you?

____

____

2) If you know Jesus, what has He done for you?

____

____

3) What do you want to do to show your appreciation and gratefulness?

____

____

____

Chapter Four

Tender Teens

"How can a young man keep his way pure?
By living according to your word."
~ Psalm 119:9

Tender Teens

At age 13, in Junior High School, I had an interesting experience that taught me a valuable lesson. I had a crush on a guy whose name was Ethan. He was quiet and attractive. One day, I let it slip and told a classmate of mine that I liked Ethan. She happened to be his cousin. After that, she wouldn't let it rest and kept trying to find ways for us to meet. Ethan was quiet and I was shy and we didn't have any classes together. I have no idea what she told her cousin, but she must have been plaguing Ethan as she was plaguing me. Remember those days? Well, one day after school she pushed me to go up to him and speak to him. I'll never forget his response. He got angry and told me to leave him alone because he didn't like me. Can you imagine the embarrassment I felt, and even more so because this was done in front of a group of Ethan's friends? I went home that day, sat in a corner and cried my eyes out for a couple of hours. I learned a valuable lesson that day and I'm glad that I learned it then and not later in life. I decided then that I would never put myself in that position again. I would "chase" no man because that's what it felt like and that was a terrible feeling. I'm glad of the outcome because today as I look at how some women who chase men appear desperate, needy and sometimes lacking self-respect; it makes me feel blessed to have had such a lesson so young in life to build upon.

I suppose I could have allowed that embarrassing situation to cause me to doubt myself, but even though I was shy, I still had healthy self-respect. It also helped that shortly after that, the guy's brother, who was a year or so older than I and much better looking than his younger brother, began pursuing me. It was an ego booster, but I just wasn't interested.

Late Teen Years…

There were five young men in particular between the ages of 17-20 that did or spoke things into my life that made an impact which I'll remember forever. Three were "boyfriends" at one time or another. One was a wanna be boyfriend, but a good friend nevertheless. The fifth was the oldest, and an acquaintance and neighbor of my cousin.

From the four who were friends, they reinforced the feeling I'd gotten from my dad that I was special, a princess, if you will. Each treated me with such respect and they weren't all Christian young men, two were and two were not. One, Jamie, even washed my foot on one occasion when I stepped in a mud puddle while we were going for a walk. My cousins and their boyfriends and Jamie and I were exploring a new housing development that had not been fully completed. None of the new houses were inhabited yet so we decided to explore the homes and dreamed of what we wanted when we grew up and got married. At some point during this exploration, the couples separated to view homes on their own. During our exploration on our own, Jamie never tried to kiss me or take advantage of the opportunity. It actually hadn't even occurred to me that that was possible until we went into one of the homes and came across one couple kissing.

As we were leaving the development, the roads had not yet been paved and were muddy from the rain the day before. It was getting dark and as Jamie and I walked and talked, I forgot to pay attention to where I was walking and stepped in a puddle. Thankfully, a standpipe wasn't far ahead, so we stopped for me to wash my foot. However, Jamie wouldn't let me do it; he washed my foot himself. That was over 20 years ago, but I remember it like it was last week. That was pretty special to me.

Two of the other young men were friends competing for my attention to become my boyfriend. The three of us hung out together at times and at other times I spent time with one or the other or together with them with a group of friends. Among them I was learning to be myself and to be free, without fear because they protected and honored me. I suppose you could say that through my relationship with them, my trust in men was being restored.

Neither of them pressured me sexually so I learned true friendship with the opposite sex. Now maybe they were responding to something in me that said, "hands off" that I might not even have been aware that I was emitting. At any rate, I'm grateful for their sensitivity and caring.

"Neither of them pressured me sexually so I learned true friendship with the opposite sex."

On the other hand, the fifth individual and the eldest of them, was somewhere between 21 and 24 years old. He chose to misuse his influence. He was but an acquaintance and during the last month I lived in Trinidad, he tried to rape me on my 15th birthday. The Lord was with me once again. On my birthday, I went to visit my cousins and at the end of the day when I was ready to go home, Will, a well-known neighbor, offered me a ride home. He was handsome and most of the girls in the neighborhood had a crush on him, however, I wasn't one of them. Though he was cute, so was his brother and his brother and I liked each other. His brother and I were also only about two years apart in age.

I had no romantic interest in Will. As I left my cousin's home to take a taxi or maxi taxi (a minivan taxi) home, Will offered me a ride home on his motorcycle and I accepted. I thought nothing of it. I was 15 years old and not only would it save me money but it would also look cool. Besides, who would have thought anything could happen. I've since learned otherwise, of course. Half way home, Will asked if it was okay to stop by a friend's home to pick up something and I said it was okay. However, instead of going to his friend's home he took me into the woods, to the back of my Junior High School. (School was on break for the summer and no one was around.) Thank God for his protection.

When I realized what he was up to and that he had no intention of taking me home until he had his way with me, as soon as the bike stopped I got off and started walking. When he realized I was serious and not interested in his advances, he said he would take me home. However, when he got close, he grabbed me, tripped me, got on top of me and attempted to kiss me and part my legs, but God was with me. There was no one around to scream to for help and I knew I couldn't fight him and win. So I simply concentrated on what I could control. I clamped my teeth shut, tightly crossed my arms over my chest and locked my feet and thighs together. He kept trying to gain access to me, but couldn't and he eventually gave up and took me home.

Thinking about it today I don't think that this guy was being malicious. He was however arrogant, conceited and selfish, thinking only of his desires. He thought all the girls wanted him, including me. I was friendly but I'd never had so much as a conversation with him that I can remember. I had no clue that he had any interest in me and maybe he didn't. Maybe he was just used to having his own way and thought I was another one he could add to his collection. He was wrong.

That experience taught me a few things and left me distrustful. It seemed like the better looking a guy was the more arrogant and assumptive he was, too. Following that experience, I took a dislike to handsome, arrogant men. I learned over the years that all handsome men are not conceited, but I met so many that were. I had to eventually learn how to effectively deal with them. I chose simply not to deal with them or got good at cutting them to the quick.

About a month and half to two months after this experience, I met Rick. I met him the week before I left Trinidad to reunite with my mom and live in the US. He seemed to be a really nice and handsome guy about seventeen years old. Rick was an electrician working on the new dorm being built for the women on the Bible school campus where I lived with my aunt. She was the dean of women. After school, I went up to the building to explore how things were going (there were no other teens on campus, so I had to find some entertainment). What a delight it was to meet Rick and talk with him while he worked. I suppose I flirted with him a little bit. I knew that I was getting ready to leave the country and who knows if I'd ever see him again. Besides, he was fine! He was slim, brown-skinned, with two dimples, a cleft chin and a great smile. He gave me his address so we could correspond. I never expected that we would correspond for the next nine years and talk every now and then long distance. That long distance romantic link and the near rape served to shield me mentally and emotionally for my first two years in the US as I went through culture shock and adjustment to life as a teenager in the US.

At age 17, I met two young men that also had an impact on my life. One was a stranger, about the age of 22-24 and the other was Mack, my neighbor, about 18 or 19 years old and the brother of one of my girlfriends. One day I was at my next door neighbor's home with my sister. My sister frequently hung out with them. I don't believe the brother lived there because I'd never seen him before. They were a Puerto Rican family and the brother apparently didn't speak much English. At one point, during the visit I went to go upstairs to use the restroom. On my way upstairs to the bathroom, this stranger, who I learned later was the neighbor's brother, cornered me and kissed me. I didn't know his name; I'd never met him before and never saw him thereafter. But what a kiss that was! I was 17 but hadn't any desire to kiss anyone. This guy came from out of nowhere, introduced me to what a kiss could be like and then I never saw him again. Thank God. It would've only meant trouble.

Shortly thereafter I met Mack. (I'd known him as my friend's brother and from school, but he and I never talked.) He had graduated the year before and from what I understand was getting into trouble. Now Mack was another fine brother. He was at least six feet, slender, dark-skinned, chisel-featured and handsome; another one all the girls liked and chased. That was reason enough for me to stay away. I thought he was another one of those conceited brothers. I got to know him a bit because I often hung out over his family's apartment with his sister. I don't remember how he and I got together and dated briefly, but I will always remember him for what he did for me.

Mack and even his sister, who was my friend, would have been considered of "the wrong crowd" especially for me. (My sister called me, "Miss Goodie-two-shoes.") They were both popular, but they smoked cigarettes and marijuana and probably consumed too much alcohol. Mind you, I was 17; his sister was about 14 and he only 18 or 19. Two memories stand out in my mind that served to validate my value as a young woman. Mack and some friends were at his house smoking pot one day while I was there. His sister was participating in this and encouraged me to do likewise. Mack saw me reach for the joint she was handing me and stopped me. He told me that it was not for me and that I wasn't that kind of girl. Mack also never tried to sleep with me during our brief relationship as I know he was in the habit of doing with his girlfriends.

Not too long after the incident of Mack preventing me from smoking pot, he and his family moved away and we lost contact. I feel like God put these angels around me to protect me, some just happen to be in the form of young men. It made me feel incredibly special but I don't believe I'm the only one for whom God does such things. He just had a particular message he wanted to send through my life of what he can do and will do for those who put their trust in him and want to live for him.

> "Men, you have such incredible power. You can choose to use your influence in the life of a young woman for good (and for God) or for evil. You have the power to shape a young woman's perception of herself, of her self image and self-confidence."

Men, you have such incredible power. You can choose to use your influence in the lives of young women for good (and for God) or for evil. You have the power to shape the perception that young women have of themselves, their self-image and their self-confidence. As a man how are you using your power? Are you using it for self-gratification or for empowerment? You know in the example above, I can see where some men would have encouraged me to smoke with them and would have seen it as an opportunity to get me to sleep with them. Honestly, I believe I would have smoked that joint if Mack hadn't stopped me, because I had smoked one before at the encouragement of his sister when he wasn't around. After Mack stopped me, however, I was never tempted to smoke a joint again.

A couple years ago I was flicking through the TV channels and came across a sitcom called *My Wife and Kids* starring Damon Wayans as the husband and father. I'd never seen the sitcom before, but then again, I rarely watch TV. Every now and then, however, when I do flick on the television I find a gem of a message like the one in this particular episode. In this episode, the teenage son brought home a young lady that was recommended to him by all the guys on the football or basketball team as a "good time." I think he was still a virgin and was hoping to change that status by sleeping with this girl that all the guys on the team had slept with.

When she walked into the room you could tell by her dress and her manner that she was a bit loose. The son was smiling widely and snickering. However, his dad didn't respond as he expected. His dad didn't encourage his behavior. Instead, his dad was very respectful to the young lady and after she left he educated his son on how to treat her with respect regardless of her past, regardless of what the other guys had done and how they treated her. The Father taught his son that the young lady was a human being, not a piece of meat. He told him that his expectations of him were higher and in essence, how to transfer those expectations to the young lady.

In the last scene something beautiful happened. Several weeks after he had been dating her, the son had invited the young lady over to his house. This time, however, when she came over she looked very different. She looked lovely, demure, happy and confident. Her dress code had changed and had become more modest. Her eyes had lost the hard edge. She had self-respect again. Because of the respect that the father and son gave her, it built up her self-esteem and she began to act differently. Because they gave her value and honor, she grew more honorable. That was a powerful episode. I hope you got the message.

What kind of influence have you had in the lives of young women thus far? Which group do you fall in? So far in your life, have you been instrumental in developing or damaging the young ladies that come into your life? Regardless of how old or how young you are, you are influencing lives around you. Just as the father and son in this sitcom impacted the life of this teenage girl and as the young men above greatly influenced the early years of my life, so you too can make an impact.

Tender Teens
Application

1) Consider, what kind of impact have you made or are making in the lives of the young women in your life?

____

____

2) What has been your motive in relation to the young men in your life?_______________________________________

____

3) Do you believe God is pleased? If not, what needs to change?____

____

Chapter Five

Who Are My Brothers?

"Sometimes being a brother is even better
than being a superhero."
~ Marc Brown

"There is a destiny that makes us brothers,
no one goes his way alone;
all that we send into the lives of others,
comes back into our own."
~ Edwin Markham

Who Are My Brothers?

I have four brothers and I love them, however, they are not the only brothers that I have, love and admire. I am not speaking of the brotherhood of man, nor just of my Christian brothers, but of those who have been brotherly to me. Jesus said in Matthew 12:48-50, "Who is my mother, and who are my brothers?" Then looking at his disciples he said, "Here are my mother and my brothers. For whoever does the will of my Father in heaven is my brother and sister and mother." I've truly been blessed to have loving brothers both inside and outside my natural family.

Growing up, my younger brother Curtis was the closest sibling to me. We are one year apart and even though he is the younger one, you would think he was my older brother the way he always looked out for me during my childhood and teen years. He was how I pictured a brother should be–protective. Today Curt is about 6 feet 2 inches, approximately 200 lbs, muscular and outgoing. But as a kid he was quiet and skinny and avoided a fight, at all costs. For him to have stepped up in my defense as he did at only 10 or 11 years old to protect me against the young adult man that was molesting me was huge. The father of the perpetrator seemed gruff most of the times to us as children and sometimes unapproachable. His son that troubled me was 19 or 20 years old. Uncle Dan could have ridiculed Curtis or thought him to be making up a story. Curt could have been beaten by the son for exposing what was going on, but whether he was aware of all this or not, he still chose to suffer any consequences to help me. That's a brother.

When we were teenagers and he had started dating, I told him, "Curt, as you go out with these girls, treat them like you treat me. They are somebody's sister, too." You are to be a brother, a protector to the women, whether they are sisters in Christ or not. That in itself may be witness enough to win some of these women to Christ. Protect, don't prey upon them."

> "You are to be a brother, a protector to the women, whether they are sisters in Christ or not. That in itself may be witness enough to win some of these women to Christ. Protect, don't prey upon them."

Curtis wasn't home much, nor was I, so I didn't get to observe how he interacted with his girlfriends. Then at age 18 or 19, he joined the Navy. After his four years with the Navy, he married and settled in Pennsylvania, so we didn't talk and visit frequently. However, I knew that if I needed him, he would be there for me.

My brother, T.A., who is six years my senior, added to the feeling of being special because he would say to me, "Nobody's good enough for you, Beaver." Then just recently he did something really sweet. For the first time ever, he tried to hook me up with a friend he thought very highly of that happened to be a judge. Both the judge and I wondered at the attempted hook up and both of us felt honored that T.A. thought highly enough of both of us to try to make a match. It was a very nice thought. But Ains, as we call him, didn't live with us after I was age 11. Shortly after my younger siblings and I went to live overseas, Ains left for the military. As a result of the age gap and distance in residence and life styles, we weren't as close as Curtis and I were, but by little things he did when he could, I knew that T.A. would do whatever he could for me if I needed him.

My other brother Roger, the eldest sibling, is one of those people who wants to be there for everybody. I believe the other two feel the same way, but Roger is most vocal to me about it. I love my brothers and this is the example of brotherhood that I've had before me. Therefore when I think of a brother in Christ, that's pretty much what I expect, someone who looks out for you both spiritually and naturally.

In my late teens God gave me a friend who helped to bring me out of my shell. His name was Barry Lorring. He became an international evangelist and a pastor. Barry did something significant in my life and was a true brother. As a result of the molestation I'd experienced and the separation from my mother, I became withdrawn emotionally. Throughout my teen years I was viewed as shy and to some, conceited (I think they just misunderstood my shyness). I didn't like to be touched. At church when people would greet and hug each other, I would cringe when they came to me. I hated to be hugged. I even hated for my mother to hug or touch me. I met Barry when I was about 16 years old. Around the age of 17 or so, I noticed he made it a point to hug me whenever he saw me. I cringed each time. He knew I didn't like it, so he did it all the more and laughed when I cringed. I'm grateful for his love and friendship because it helped to break down the mistrust and ice around my heart. Remember, the young man back home who molested me was a Christian. I forgot to mention that after we'd left that family my sisters and brother and I were split up for a couple years. I went to live with my aunt who was dean of women at a Bible college. My youngest sister went to stay with my uncle and aunt and the other two with another aunt and uncle. While I lived with my aunt I had another uncomfortable experience with one of the Bible school students. I say uncomfortable, because I don't remember what the man did to make me feel uncomfortable or unsafe around him. It was so long ago. He was twenty-something and I was 14 years old. However I remember how he made me feel. So I wasn't trusting of any man, sad to say. Regardless of whether he said he was a Christian or pastor, I didn't trust him.

To further the case that was building against Christian men, I had a couple more uncomfortable experiences. One was with a man who was giving me music lessons and the other from one who was practically a stranger to me but well known to the church. What do I mean by uncomfortable? Well, the music teacher's compliments and closeness during the lessons were sometimes uncomfortable. Maybe I was just sensitive due to my past, but I wasn't uncomfortable with all men. Something about him made me uncomfortable. Then there was another brother in Christ, who I had met maybe once or twice before, he came out to my car one day to greet me as I was leaving his cousin's home. Again, I barely knew him; I knew more about him than to say I knew him personally. He came over to my car and leaned into the window to hug me; I guess and somehow rubbed the back of his arm across my breast. It was an awkward movement to make, and not an accident. Both these men were Christians. On another occasion, I went to visit a family friend. The father was coming out of the garage door as I was about to enter. He was much older, maybe in his late forties or early fifties and I'd known him since I was a child. I hugged him in greeting and as he was releasing me from the hug, he decided to give me a big wet kiss on my mouth. Yuck! He too, was a Christian. It's a wonder I didn't give up altogether on men in the church.

Barry helped improve my view of Christian men, as did my pastor, Pastor Edgar Billings who acted as a surrogate father. Barry knew exactly what he was doing every time he hugged me. He saw the walls I'd built up and was doing his part to tear them down and show me the love of Christ. In later years, I brought that up to Barry and he admitted that he knew that I was very uncomfortable with him hugging me and that's why he purposely did so. I'm glad he did. I've used the same tactic with many youth when I became a youth minister. I had to be careful, being a young, single female, but I too saw very shy teenage girls and boys come out of their shell as I hugged on them, spent time with them and invested my life in them.

Pastor Billings was also such a blessing. He looked out for me and became my protector. Any young man that came to our church and cast his glance at me, Pastor grilled him, gave him the eye, or flexed, or so it seemed to me. At any rate, I felt protected. I thank the Lord for looking out for me by placing these men in my life.

These men, these brothers and fathers in Christ modeled the following instruction that Paul gave to Timothy so long ago; the foundation for relationships in the body of Christ, "…exhort him (an older man) as if he were your father. Treat younger men as brothers, older women as mothers, and younger women as sisters, with absolute purity" (1 Timothy 5:1, 2).

This principle of brotherly love is sadly lacking in instruction and application in many churches today. It needs to be taught more at home and in church. The conversations I've had with many single, Christian women on an individual basis as well as in group settings would indicate that many women do not feel they are being treated "as sisters, with absolute purity."

Rather, many have been hurt, feel used and have become almost cynical. Where's the brotherly love? Does it always have to be about courtship or dating? We all have needs for companionship and desires for sex at some point. I agree with scripture that when a man finds a wife he finds a good thing. But how many women do you date or befriend on average before you actually find your wife? That is for those who are searching, as opposed to those who are waiting for God to reveal their wife. How are you searching? How are you treating these women in your pursuit of a mate? Is it with respect, honor and recognition that their body is the temple of the Holy Spirit? Do you recognize that if she's not the one then she belongs to another and that your future wife may be involved in the same scenario with someone else? How would you like for her to be treated while she is waiting for you to find her? 1Thessalonians 4:3-6 talks about how we are to conduct ourselves under these circumstances. It says, "It is God's will that you should be sanctified: that you should avoid sexual immorality; that each of you should learn to control his own body in a way that is holy and honorable, not in passionate lust like the heathen, who do not know God; and that in this matter no one should wrong his brother or take advantage of him."

"How are you searching [for a wife]? How are you treating these women in your pursuit of a mate? Is it with respect, honor and recognition that their body is the temple of the Holy Spirit?"

About 21 years ago, I briefly dated a guy named Ian. He was fresh out of college and a fervent believer. (You'll hear a little more about Ian in a later chapter.) I guess he was a little taken aback when I didn't comply with his version of dating. He'd gone to a prominent secular college and told me that while he was in college it was normal for the Christian couples there to become intimate without actually having sexual intercourse. Since I hadn't been to college yet and he had graduated top of his class and had been the class president, I suppose I seemed uneducated, unsophisticated and backward. Who was I to think I was "better" than them by refusing to engage in such practices?

That was over twenty years ago. I can only imagine what it's like today on college campuses. Again, not enough is being taught on this subject, which when you consider the world we live in today with rampant sexual immorality within and outside the church, this has got to become an area of focus and teaching in the body of Christ. We hear, "live holy," but how? We hear "avoid sexual immorality," but how in today's culture? I thank God that he has protected me and given me wisdom in dealing with men throughout my life. He taught me how to treat them as brothers and, importantly, how to win them over as brothers and friends. But that's not going to be many women. Most are waiting for you to take the lead as a man and show them how a man can control his own body in holiness and in honor. But even more importantly, can you show her honor? Can you deny yourself? Can you overlook her ignorance or lack of self-respect and give her respect- because after all, she is a vessel for which Christ died?

I have such great respect for men who've learned and apply this principle. It takes discipline. It takes a renewing of the mind. It takes self-denial. It takes prayer and fasting. It takes wisdom. It takes courage. It takes a real man.

Who Are My Brothers?
Application

1) Who are some of the women in your circle that you are being a brother to? Name some of them?

____

____

2) What are you doing that indicates you are treating them as a true brother?

____

____

3) Is Christ lifted up in those relationships?

____

____

Chapter Six

The Turning Point

"It is never too late to become
what you might have been."
~ George Eliot

The Turning Point

There were several young men during my young adult years that further contributed to my development as a young woman. Like a house being built, brick upon brick, so were their lives bricks in the building of my femininity. From age 19 to 21, I strayed from faith in Christ. I was discouraged with some of my Christian friendships, felt betrayed by some of them and withdrew from our church and my Christian associates at that time. I started going to clubs from Friday to Sunday. I simply loved to dance; it was my outlet but I thank God that he gave me some wisdom on how to handle myself during that time and I thank him for keeping me while going through that period of rebellion.

I still didn't date much, I really only wanted to go out, dance and have a good time. I wasn't looking for any relationships, wasn't interested in alcohol, drugs or sex. Even though I was a little angry with the Lord, I wasn't totally stupid. I knew my lapse was only temporary. I just loved to dance and since we were not allowed to dance at my church, I was getting my fill.

Ninety-nine percent of the time when I went to the clubs, I went with my cousin Derek who always looked out for me and acted as my protector. Other times I went out with friends. A few times I went with someone I dated. My primary intent was simply to lose myself in the music. During that time in my life, I briefly dated a couple of young men I actually met via the clubs. Each tried to seduce me, but did not push me when I said no to sex. Brett and Henry may not even remember me, but I'm grateful they respected me enough to honor my stand. I don't know why they chose to honor my decision considering I had gotten myself into some pretty compromising situations with each of them. They could easily have said to themselves, "She led me on," to justify pursuing intercourse. But they didn't. Was it their background or upbringing? Was it simply God's intervention? Was it that I was adamant? It could have been all of the above. I'm just grateful they were the kind of men that they were and thankful for God's protection even while I was rebelling against him.

Then one Saturday night I reached my turning point. I went to visit my cousins in Hartford, CT, about forty minutes away from my home in Springfield, MA. Only this evening, that I wanted to go out dancing, Derek was nowhere to be found. So I went with his sister and her boyfriend, still feeling somewhat safe. It wasn't the same though, some time during the evening they had left me at the club.

> 'That night while on the dance floor I heard a voice behind me say, "What if Jesus came back tonight, what would happen to you?" I turned around and no one was there."

At this point in my rebellion against the Lord, the whole club scene was starting to get a bit stale. That night, while on the dance floor, I heard a voice behind me say, "What if Jesus came back tonight, what would happen to you?" I turned around and no one was there. I was a bit shook up, but not enough to stop dancing for a little while longer. I finally sat down trying to decide what to do. I was alone, it was late and I had not driven. Then I noticed the man sitting next to me looking a bit sad. We struck up a conversation. He was basically drowning his sorrows with alcohol because he had recently broken up with his girlfriend. We talked the rest of the evening. It turns out he was one of the owners of the club. When it was time for the club to close I felt a little lost. I'd never been in that position before where neither family nor friend was present and I didn't have transportation.

The young man, whose name I don't recall, offered to give me a ride to my aunt's home. Once in his car, he invited me to see his penthouse downtown and said afterwards he'd give me a ride to my aunt's. I really was naïve. I honestly didn't think he was interested in me since he'd just been crying on my shoulder for the last couple hours about his ex-girlfriend. I didn't think I had anything to fear, but I soon learned differently. Once at his penthouse, he offered me wine, cheese and crackers and turned on the television. He turned the television to a pornographic channel. When I said I didn't watch that kind of programming he flicked the channels for a bit then returned it to a porn channel again and again. Then he came onto me hard and tried to remove my clothing. As we would say back home, "I high-tailed it out of there!" I let him know that I was not sexually active nor was I interested in becoming so, ran out of the penthouse and started walking in the direction I thought would lead me to my aunt's house. He proceeded to follow me, driving alongside, apologizing for his behavior. He offered to take me home. It was about 3:00 a.m. and I had no business walking in the street at that hour. I took a chance and got in his car and true to his word he did take me to my aunt's. I don't know what I would've done if he hadn't. I had no money with me, didn't know where I was, and this was around 1989 when cell phones were not yet common. I got out of that car and never looked back. That was my turning point.

The next day began our church's annual camp meeting conference. I went down to the church altar and rededicated my life to the Lord. Thank God for His mercy and grace that kept me during my rebellious interlude. The outcome could have been so very different if it wasn't for his grace and mercy. My heart wasn't really out there in the world. I knew my place and I knew the goodness of God. I found nothing out there to compare to God's goodness or that could fill the void or warm my heart like his Holy Spirit. So, like the prodigal son, I ran home.

What about you? Have you reached your turning point or crossroads? God is good. He pursues us even when we are not looking for him. He pursues us even when we don't want him. He loves us yet he allows us to wander and to do our own thing. But if you belong to him, he won't let you wander out of reach of his grace. He's always standing right behind you waiting for you to turn to Him.

.

Turning Point
Application

1) Are you walking in disobedience or rebellion in any area of your life? If so, what is it?

____

____

2) How does it feel? Are you tired yet?

____

____

3) What would happen to you if death came unexpectedly before you had a chance to turn back to God? Be honest with yourself, what would happen to you and what legacy would you leave for your children or family to follow?

____

____

Chapter Seven

Friendship Training

"Hold a true friend with both your hands."
~ Nigerian Proverb

Friendship Training

Twenty-something....

About a year or two after I had rededicated my life to the Lord, my buddy Barry introduced me to a friend of his from college, whose name was Kevin. Barry brought him home during their summer break. They were in Bible school together. Several years later, Kevin became my fiancé, but when we first met I thought him to be an arrogant, posturing, boisterous upstart. He was indeed conceited. He was twenty four years old and I was twenty two. All the young ladies catered to him. He didn't impress me, however, as he wasn't my type. He was about 5 feet, 10 inches, with dark brown skin tone, about 200-210 lbs, stocky rather than slender, bow-legged, always with a grin on his face. He walked very self-assured and his conversation was often peppered with long syllable words. We were thrown together a lot because Barry and a few of our friends spent a great deal of time together. Maybe I caught his eye because I was one of the only females who wasn't impressed with him and had no desire for his company. He started to pursue me, and though at first I really wasn't interested, his persistence paid off and I agreed to go out with him. We were like oil and water, but during that time I learned a great deal from him.

We only dated for maybe 10 months to a year and most of that time he was away at college. Even though we didn't have a lot of time together, in the time we did have together, Kevin made a huge impact on my life. He wasn't used to a shy but assured young woman like myself and I wasn't used to a loud, arrogant, roughneck like him. I didn't really take him seriously at first, because we were so different and I had never met anyone like him. Though he was quite rough, like an uncut diamond, I learned from him. He taught me how to drive a stick shift car. He taught me about myself through our conversations and it was actually he that made me begin to feel comfortable with my femininity. It's weird, but even though I was a young woman, I didn't know much about my own body. I hadn't thought too much about it really and I didn't hang around with females growing up so I wasn't privy to the normal girly conversations where some of those blanks might have been filled in or my interest to learn more piqued. Hanging with Kevin who was really the first adult man with whom I became intimately connected, I started to unfold.

Before Kevin, I had been physically intimate with the two other young men mentioned previously, Brett and Henry, whom I dated briefly. I was physically intimate as far as kissing and sexual foreplay, but it was all physical. I was not emotionally involved or even very interested in the physical intimacy. My body was being addressed and undressed, but neither my mind nor my heart was moved. I was simply going through the motions, up to a point, and when it got to the point of penetration, I withdrew. So I was physically intimate, but not truly intimate with either of them. They didn't know me. I didn't have any real mental or emotional interaction with them. All I remember is that we partied a few times and then they tried to sleep with me. However, Brett did introduce me to football and the whole sports scene. Thank God both interludes were semi-long distance relationships. Brett lived about an hour away, and Henry lived two hours away. Both lasted only a couple months.

In stark contrast, Kevin came into my life after I had rededicated my life to Christ. He encouraged me to keep myself pure. He didn't pressure me sexually, he didn't even try to kiss me until about the fifth month we were dating and even then, he asked me. This impressed me greatly and affected how I viewed every man that approached me thereafter. This conceited, intelligent but boisterous roughneck, though still young in his faith, showed me more love, sensitivity and respect by his treatment of me than many of the educated, polished, Christianized men, both young and old, that pursued me over the years. We remained friends throughout the years, and six years after we'd first dated, we got engaged. When the relationship didn't work out, he told me in his rough way, "Keep a quarter squeezed tightly between your knees." In other words, don't let any man get between my knees. Even when we were engaged he protected my purity. That's a man I could respect and he set a standard for me.

A few months after Kevin and I broke up, a sharp guy named Ian that I mentioned briefly in a previous chapter started attending our church. Being the hospitable person that I'd developed into, I introduced myself to him. I'd changed so much that I now always introduce myself to visitors at church whether, man woman or child. I want them to feel at home and welcome in our sanctuary. I could tell he thought I was being a little forward and probably thought I was interested in him. But I didn't pay that any mind. My rational was that as time went by, he would quickly learn that I was just being friendly and appreciated intelligent conversation from someone whose spirit said, "I love the Lord" louder than his voice, and his did that.

Ian and I became friends and I learned several things from him. Now even though others may have found him physically attractive, I did not at all. On the contrary, I actually found him unattractive. In fact, I think he was a bit taken aback that I did not display any interest in him other than friendship. I simply enjoyed his company. There was something, in particular, that I learned from our time of friendship. I was learning, as an adult how to be friends with the opposite sex. I'll never forget the wonderful times we had that summer going to a local national park, spreading out a blanket and studying the Word of God together. That was simply priceless to me. Or after church Sunday evenings dissecting the messages and sharing what God was saying to each of us. It was fantastic. It opened my eyes to the possibilities I could have in a relationship. Several months later, Ian decided he wanted to court me. I remember praying, "Lord, please make him appear attractive to me if this is your will." We did end up in a brief courtship, but once again, he was another one, who as a Christian didn't uphold a high standard of purity. So once the relationship began to move in a direction that repeatedly threatened to compromise my standard of purity, we separated and neither of us attempted to keep in contact.

Shortly after this experience I took a trip to Guatemala for a Spanish immersion course. I felt called into missions and wanted to go to Mexico as a missionary one day. So prior to going away to Bible school, I went, on my own, to Guatemala. It was quite an adventure, but interestingly enough, once again most of the friends I made there were men. I studied in Guatemala for three months. I was tutored one on one by a man who spoke no English. The family I lived with spoke no English. They housed two other students, as well, who were both men. The first friend I made there was a guy from Switzerland. He was hiking through Central America. He took me touring my first few days in Guatemala, and then he was on his way. Later, I joined a group of other Europeans; most of them were men, as well. I really thought nothing of it. They took me into their circle, showed me around and provided companionship. I felt completely safe the entire time and enjoyed the whole cultural and educational experience.

When I reflect on my life at this point, I see that I actually gravitate more to male friendships. I like their straightforwardness, the way they think and the covering or protection most of them offer. I want to be protected and look for it in a man regardless of their position in my life; I expect it no matter where I am. It makes me feel ultra-feminine and I almost want to say that I feel that it's my right by virtue of being the physically weaker sex to expect the men in my life to protect me.

"I want to be protected and look for it in a man regardless of their position in my life. I expect it no matter where I am. It makes me feel ultra-feminine and I almost want to say that I feel that it's my right by virtue of being the physically weaker sex to expect the men in my life to protect me."

Unfortunately, in society today, being an independent, single, self-sufficient woman seems synonymous with being hard, pushy, forward and sometimes even masculine. Well here's my philosophy, a single woman on her own, has to be independent or self-sufficient in America or we find ourselves to be prey.

In America, women have largely lost their protective covering due to a number of things. First, culturally, women no longer stay in their parents' home until they marry. (In many countries, around the world today, it is still the practice for the women to stay at home with their parents until they marry.)

Many years ago, when a young woman left her father's household, she left his covering to enter marriage and therefore entered under the new covering of her husband. Now however, most leave the covering of their parents' home and go out on their own seeking independence, higher education or a career and then marry later.

Second, a large number of women come from single parent homes due to divorce, abandonment, separation or premarital pregnancies. (This may be the second or third generation of single parenting in some of their families.) The covering in this example comes from the female since the father wasn't there to do his job. Many of the girls who grow into womanhood from this environment don't know anything else but a fight for survival and equality. There might not have been a male figure in their life to provide protection except for an older brother or other relative.

Third, the creation of the African American culture created independent and strong African American women. By design, the slave trade that brought the African people here to America created broken families and made breeding stock of both men and women. The women by virtue of their forced environment had to become independent and strong to survive and protect their children.

Their environment and cultural expectations breed and promote independence and self-sufficiency. The men in return treat these self-assured, successful, independent women like men and not like the softer, gentler sex in need of protection, care and provision. When they try, many of the independent women don't know how to receive it and thus reject it. I think many women want the protection and care but don't know how to receive it. Some reject it as foreign because it's unfamiliar to their experiences. By the time they realize what it is and want to accept it; the men have already withdrawn the offers. It's a vicious cycle, one that needs to be understood and corrected if change is desired.

Lessons from College....

When I returned from Guatemala, I went away to Bible school in Minnesota. That was a beautiful time in my life. I learned so much more than what was taught in the classroom. I didn't realize that I had developed a cynical view of marriage. Most of the marriages that I'd seen, up to that point, were dysfunctional and not encouraging. Bethany College of Missions was a very unique college because of its focus, the way it was founded and its communal format. The students and faculty lived on the campus together and worked together outside of the classroom. Bethany housed Bethany House Publishers and a printing company. The businesses were run by the staff and students. We got to observe the staff families up close and I witnessed so many amazing marriages, young and old. They gave me hope. They showed me examples of healthy relationships, young and old, that let me know that marriages really can work.

There were three marriages in particular; I was able to observe over a two-year period while working in the publicity department. My supervisor had been married for over 30 years by that time and I often saw her and her husband hold hands as they walked. I never heard or witnessed them argue. The other two couples were the marketing director and his assistant. They were both in their thirties. Sean, the director, was a wonderful guy, in his late 30's or early 40's, handsome and always cheerful. He also wore the best cologne, subtle and sexy. All of us women in the office talked about it. He was always appropriate in his communication with the employees. Sean always talked lovingly about his wife. I never met her, never saw them together, but it's just the way he spoke of her after several years of marriage. They had a teen daughter so I knew they'd been married for awhile, yet, he was obviously still in love with his wife.

Then there was Sean's assistant Danielle. She couldn't have been more than 30 or 32, athletic build, beautiful blond, and always smiling. Danielle had two adolescent children and a husband that would come and meet her for lunch at least once or twice a week or meet her after work so they could walk home together (remember we all lived on a small campus). Some evenings or weekends I'd see the family riding their bikes on campus or in the park. They were always together. Danielle told me that she and David married right after they graduated from high school and by the looks of things, were able to maintain their young love throughout their married life. Sadly, David died suddenly a few years ago of an aneurysm. At least, by that time, they'd had over twenty happy years of marriage.

During my first semester as a freshman at Bethany, the Lord told me not to date. It was one Sunday after church as I was doing some leisure reading. The book was either *A Higher Call* or *Shepherd of the Hills* both by Harold Bell Wright and published by Bethany. I read them one after the other so I don't remember after which it was that I was led to stop dating. Both are works of fiction, but have strong, challenging messages of truth. When I finished reading this particular book, I was moved to my knees and prayer. It was during that time of prayer that I felt the Holy Spirit telling me not to date. He didn't say for how long, just that I shouldn't date. Neither book had anything to do with dating, per se. They fell in the category of drama or romance. The message was similar in both books. The one I remember the most, still have today, and that possibly had the most impact on me is, *A Higher Call*. It's about a young pastor who challenges the perspective of the twentieth-century church and runs into a lot of opposition and hypocrisy in his church. A quote on the front cover of the book should give you a good idea of the content: "You have let go of the commands of God and are holding on to the traditions of men."

After my session of prayer, following the reading of the book, I gave up dating. Now any time you make a decision like that, you can expect it to be tested immediately. The next semester and over the summer I had at least five men approach me who were interested in either courtship or dating me, only two of which I'll share about in any detail. I believe that because of this experience and my commitment to refrain from dating that I was able to do some healthy self analysis as well as learn to develop healthy friendships with men.

At Bethany I met two young men in particular that God used to take me to another level in my life and walk with the Lord. The first was Karl. Karl was from Canada and he was only at our college for one semester. He was part of an association from Canada that had a group of missionaries in training to participate in one semester at our school prior to going on an overseas mission's internship. What a breath of fresh air Karl was! We had a lot of fun and fellowship together. Karl had a shy way about him, but was very funny, attractive, intelligent and in love with Jesus. We met because we had a few classes together and sat next to each other a few times. We struck up a friendship that was easygoing and carefree. I felt I could totally be myself with him. In the morning before class I would sometimes go to the chapel or find an empty classroom to pray and worship. Several times when I'd finished, I had found Karl at the entry way watching me. We both loved nature and would take long walks even in the bitter Midwestern cold and snow. We were like two kids and we had a lot of fun.

One day a couple months after we'd been hanging out with each other, Karl made it clear that he was interested in courting me. It was at that time that I had a moment of revelation about myself. Even though I found Karl attractive in many ways, on many levels, and really liked him and enjoyed his company immensely, I suddenly realized two important things. First, we did not have compatible callings. God had called Karl to Eastern Europe and called me to stay in the inner city of the US. Therefore, God wasn't putting us together for marriage. Secondly, I noticed that when I've been attracted or interested in men, I only seem to stay interested for about four weeks before the attraction starts to wane. I told him this and suggested we continue as we were without a commitment to a relationship then for him to ask me again after a month or so to see if I was still interested. Sure enough, he introduced the subject again five weeks later and though I still immensely enjoyed his company, admired him and cared for him, my attraction had definitely begun to wane.

I believe God has created each of us differently and for a definite purpose. We are each specially wired for God's purposes, not that that means that we all walk in his purposes or that we walk in them every day. I think of God's words to Jeremiah: "Before I formed you in the womb I knew you, before you were born I set you apart; I appointed you as a prophet to the nations," Jeremiah 1:5. Then in Ephesians 1:4-5, the Bible says,

"For he chose us in him before the creation of the world to be holy and blameless in his sight. In love he predestined us to be adopted as his sons through Jesus Christ…" Then in the same chapter, verse 11 says, "In him we were also chosen, having been predestined according to the plan of him who works out everything in conformity with the purpose of his will…" Abraham was predestined. Moses was no accident, nor was David, Solomon, Ruth, Rahab, Judas, John the Baptist, or you and me.

What if all these experiences in my life, so far mentioned, were predestined? Or at least the occurrences were? They all had a role in my development and the birth of this testimony, right? Having surrendered my life to Jesus at a young age, being guided by him from a young age, giving him permission to take my life and use it at a young age, could he not have placed these men in my life purposely for me to tell this story, to bring him glory, to impact wondering and wandering lives? Our lives are to be living epistles, lived as an example to others, a living book for others to read about God's wondrous ways, his glory and his power. Our lives are no longer our own once we surrender them to Christ, no matter at what age this is done. "Do you not know that your body is a temple of the Holy Spirit, who is in you, whom you have received from God? You are not your own; you were bought at a price…" (1 Corinthians 6:19, 20). I can't say that I've always been obedient since God saved me at age 12. We all fall short, but even in how we handle our failure, we can be an example.

I've recently been told that I am complicated. I suppose that could be true, but could it also be that I just know who I am, what I want, what I need and know my purpose? If you aim at nothing, you'll hit it every time. But if you have a specific aim and practice shooting at it, aren't you more likely to hit it? A friend and mentor of mine, Walter Charles, has a saying, "When purpose is not known, misuse is inevitable." There is general purpose and specific purpose for each individual. I believe the general purpose is constant, but the specific purpose can be both constant and seasonal. For example, a general purpose is that we were all created to worship God. We are created to bring glory to his name. That is a general purpose which remains constant. It will not change.

An example of a specific purpose is my friendship with Karl. He came into my life sixteen and half years ago. I don't know if he learned anything from our encounter, but God used him in my life to begin to reveal to me this concept of general and specific purpose and how important it is for me to understand his purpose for my life. I have not spoken or communicated with Karl in 10 or more years. God placed him in my life for a specific purpose or for a season to teach me some things about myself, about men, and about God. Just before we left for school vacation that year, which was going to be the last time I would see Karl, he took the time to prepare a cassette for me of songs that talked about friendship and what our friendship meant to him. It was incredibly special and a blessing throughout the years. I could have easily become involved with Karl. Most of the right elements of attraction and compatibility were there except, of course, what I've learned to be the most important element–God's will, God's purpose and plan. In that area, we were not compatible for marriage.

Shortly after Karl left our college, the Lord brought another man into my life that cemented the lesson the Lord was teaching me. I was instantly attracted to Gregory and the attraction had absolutely nothing to do with his physical appearance and everything to do with his spirit. Why do I say that? Gregory's physical appearance was not what would normally attract me. I like men with a very dark complexion, tall, slender and with hair on their heads. Gregory was Caucasian, chubby and balding on top. But he had a smile that lit up the room and a spirit that drew you into the presence of the Lord.

I first saw Gregory in one of our chapel services on campus. When I walked into chapel that morning, service had already started. As I walked in, Gregory was sitting on a stool on the platform playing his classical guitar, singing and worshiping God. He had just returned from a two year mission's internship overseas and he was our guest speaker that morning. I don't remember what he sang or what he said, all I remember was the aura that was around him, the love for God that emitted from him and I immediately wanted to get to know this humble and open man that was so obviously in love with Jesus. I didn't meet him that day or right away. I was invited to a small birthday party on campus one day and he was there. We were introduced and made an immediate connection. I wanted to learn how to play the guitar and Gregory volunteered to teach me. We began to meet weekly for guitar lessons and then he and I began singing together. We didn't have a lot of time to spend together, but somehow we'd made a deep connection. So much so that Gregory asked me to join with him and go overseas as missionaries to an Asian country. Now as much as I would have liked to go, for I dearly wanted to be an overseas missionary, and Asia fascinated me, I knew, however, that God had called me to stay in the US to work in the inner-city. Therefore, I knew Gregory was not the one for me despite the deep attraction and bond we'd established. So I let go.

Thirty-Something …

As I mentioned, the Lord called me to inner-city missions. He led me to Maryland to do what I thought was going to be an internship for two years with an internationally focused missions church just outside of Washington, DC. That "internship" lasted 10 years. We worked with refugees from Cambodia, Vietnam, and Ethiopia, parts of Central America, other African countries and a few Americans. It was fascinating working intimately with so many different cultures. We preached and taught the Word of God, taught English as a second language, provided food, ministered to the homeless in DC, and acted as a liaison for parents to the school system. I didn't have a lot of time for a social life, and didn't feel a driving need to be in a relationship most of the time. Nevertheless, I developed several friendships with men during that time that have also made a lasting impression.

Now there's something I failed to mention that occurred just after I graduated from Bethany. I was still on campus for the summer, working at Bethany House Publishers in the publicity department. Something happened one morning that subsequently affected my attitude towards men.

One morning at about, 8:30 a.m. while at work, I got a phone call. The male voice on the other end greeted me then proceeded to tell me that he'd just had a dream about me and called me as soon as he woke up. Maybe that's why I didn't immediately recognize the voice, because it was his sleepy voice, I don't know. So I asked, "Who is this?" (I thought maybe somebody on campus was playing a joke on me.) He replied, "Kevin!" as though I should have known. Mind you, I had not spoken with him in at least six months. (Kevin is the guy that I'd dated for about 10 months and we were like oil and water…) I don't remember anymore what the dream was about, but I remember how the conversation ended and the effect the encounter has had on my decisions ever since. The two primary things I remember from our conversation were, one, that he'd started working with teenagers (he's a counselor) and two, I remember his typical closing question, "Will you marry me?" As usual I laughed it off without giving an actual answer, not believing he could be serious considering we hadn't been together or even seen each other in about five years. I was not aware that my supervisor was listening to my conversation.

Shortly after I got off the phone, my supervisor asked me what was so funny. I proceeded to tell her why I was laughing. She looked at me seriously and asked why that was funny? I told her that of all the people on earth, Kevin was the least likely person I'd marry. She probed further to find out why? Well, I said, besides the fact that he's a rough-neck, coarse, crude and not my type, he's backslidden. She still looked at me as though I hadn't said anything reasonable. I said it would be impossible or would take a miracle. She replied, "Isn't the God we serve, the God of miracles and the God of impossibilities?" I was disturbed and stumped.

The conversation with my supervisor troubled me for the rest of the morning. I could hardly focus, it was bothering me so. When lunch time came I went to my dorm room and prayed, because for some reason, her words resonated in my spirit and I started to think that maybe God was speaking to me through her. While I prayed, I got the conviction that this man was God's choice for me and that I was to wait. I remember saying at the end of that season of prayer, "Father, if this is you, then however long it takes for you to bring us together I expect that he will not have married (and divorced), not have had any children, and of course since we can't be unequally yoked, he will have returned to you and be serving you." When I got up from my knees I felt peace, though, I had a growing feeling of incredibility.

After this experience, I believed Kevin was going to be my husband and told those who approached me seeking a romantic relationship as much, but I certainly wasn't going to tell Kevin this breaking news. During my second year in Maryland, Kevin called me and told me he'd rededicated his life to the Lord, was full of excitement and then asked me to marry him. I agreed, not because I was in love with him. I hadn't seen him in six years and communication with him was infrequent. There was, however, a bond between the two of us that I couldn't explain. His proposal was over the phone and I accepted because I felt I was being obedient to the Lord.

Now let me clarify. I didn't pray about it when he asked me to find out if the timing was the Lord's. I just agreed because I believe the Lord had told me this man would be my husband and he now met the basic requirements I'd requested. We were engaged for about a year. It was a bit rocky, he backslid again and I left. During the time together I'd learned to love him deeply, but we were just on two different paths. I did what I felt was right by breaking off the engagement, but it was extremely painful. I cried myself to sleep for about six months. When we broke up he'd said to me, "Don't you feel like you are bone of my bone and flesh of my flesh?" I did, but God forgive me, I lied and said no. I didn't want to admit to him that I felt the same way and make the separation more difficult. I just knew I couldn't marry him at that time.

A few months later I was introduced to a young man named Tevon on my job. I'd started working part-time with the YMCA as a director of one of their outreach centers in the same community of refugees where I was already ministering. Tevon had just taken a post as a youth minister at a neighboring church and was enlisted to help as a mentor to teenage boys in a county program. Our two agencies collaborated on youth programs and we started working together. Over the next couple of years Tevon became one of my closest friends. He was like a brother.

We could talk about anything–prayed together, and hung out together. He was a guest speaker for our youth ministry, and helped me whenever I needed help with anything. Tevon is one of my best friends for life. What a balm he was during that time shortly after my break up with Kevin.

My friendship with Tevon (Von) played a key role in helping to further develop my positive outlook on men and a natural, unpretentious relationship with the opposite sex. With Von, I felt I could be myself and be safe, not preyed upon. He was a gentleman, honest, always respectful, fun and godly. Then God moved him back to Florida. My companion was gone.

I took up roller skating for release and to meet some people socially. There I encountered three other men, one of them was Tony. Tony was a sweetheart and became like a big brother to me. He was always looking out for me. He had such a gentle nature and an intense desire to live for God and please Him. He is the kind of person who would give you the shirt off his back if he felt you needed it more than he did. We hung out now and then, mostly at the skating rink, or with some of his friends and sometimes at my place. When they came over, they automatically would go to the kitchen to see if there was anything on the stove for them to eat. That's just how we rolled. Whether it was one of my dancer students, a teen from the youth group, Tevon, or Tony and his entourage, they all felt at home enough to go to the kitchen and find themselves something to eat.

Everybody you meet has a special place in your life. Tony was like a bridge in mine. He helped me over some things and situations and I appreciate him. God also used him to continue the building up of my trust in men.

To complete my "friendship education" with the opposite sex, Raul came into my life and became one of my best friends and the inspiration for this book. When I think of Raul, I think of a balm, someone soothing, but he was also fun and intelligent. I can't say enough about him. I wish every woman had a friend like Raul in their life. I wish there were more young men like him, respectful, gentlemanly, honest, and fun without everything leading to sex. Raul and I met at work and we connected because of our Caribbean backgrounds and culture. Our offices were close together so we talked off and on throughout the day. Then we started having lunch together and progressed to hanging out on the weekends. Raul's a handsome Haitian brother, quite a gentleman sporting a great French accent, so what woman wouldn't be attracted to him? When things, however, seemed to be moving in a romantic direction, during prayer one day, the Lord told me as clear as day, "STOP!" He actually showed me a stop sign and said, "Don't go any further, Raul is only going to be a friend." I was very grateful for that direction early on in our friendship. I shared this revelation with Raul and he honored it. Now I'm going to share with you how Raul and I interacted, which was unlike any other interaction I had with most of my male friends and why I have such a high regard for him.

Every now and then Raul would hold my hand, but primarily to help me over rough ground or stepping off a sidewalk to cross a street, almost as you would with a child or a pregnant woman. It was a tender, gentlemanly thing that he did to show caring and respect. A few months after we'd been hanging out together, we were on our way to a co-worker's home for a Halloween party up north. On our way we were about to pass one of my favorite hiking and scenic spots and I wanted to show it to him. So we stopped and hiked up the mountain to the lookout spot. Then on impulse, we decided to hike the trail. We were unprepared, with no flashlight and got stuck up on the mountain in the dark. It was a cloudy night so we couldn't read the signs on the trees and went around and around on the mountain top for a while. Every now and then the moon would peek out from behind the clouds and illuminate the way a little. I was comfortable and felt totally safe with him up there, knowing he would find a way out, but even if he didn't, I knew there was nothing to fear. I just knew he would take care of me. So I didn't question his direction, and I didn't complain about us being lost. At one point we sat down and I remember thinking, "If we have to stay here all night, I know we'll be alright."

It felt great being able to trust someone so completely. Raul was probably quietly praying for direction and eventually we did find our way out. He remarked in the car, "You know what was incredible? You didn't complain not one time or try to tell me what to do or which way to go." He said that was incredible. "Most women would have been complaining about the situation the whole time." I didn't complain or try to lead because I just knew he had it. I knew I could trust him to figure it out because I knew that he didn't depend just on his own wisdom. I knew he also had the guidance and wisdom of the Holy Spirit to aid him. The thing is when a woman knows that a man has her best interest at heart, that he respects her, cares about her, will not try to take advantage of her, when she's in a vulnerable situation and the man walks by faith in Christ, then it's easy to trust him. That combination makes it easy to submit.

It was nothing for me to watch a movie with Raul, half way curl up with him or at least put my head on his shoulder and honestly, not think anything beyond that. That's the same way I treated my brother. We were so at ease with one another and understood our roles in each other's lives that even the day he told me that he got engaged, he and I were walking arm in arm downtown taking in the sights in DC. I looked down at our linked arms and said, "Raul, you know we can't hang out like this anymore. We certainly can't walk arm in arm. Anyone watching just wouldn't understand and could misinform your new fiancé." He was so funny, because at first he started to reject the thought, not ready to accept the change.

Some of you may attempt to define my friendship with Raul as a dating relationship, however, just because we spent a lot of time together that first year we met and were attracted to each other does not mean we were dating. Dating to me implies romance, an exclusive relationship, possibly even an introductory level of intimacy, such as holding hands, walking arms around each other as lovers tend to, or even kissing. Our companionship did not involve any of the above. Raul held my hand only to assist me, not to connect with me. We walked arm in arm only once that I can remember and it was as I would walk with my sister or brother.

Remember when we were little children how we interacted with the opposite sex with a sense of neutrality? We recognized the differences between our sexes and treated each other with respect for our strengths and limitations, played together and enjoyed each other's company without a "dating" mentality. Who said that once we became adults we could no longer enjoy one another's company without dating, even if attracted to each other? It takes a specific mindset, conditioning and discipline to acknowledge to yourself and to each other that you're attracted to each other, but then choose to remain friends.

You may say, "What's the purpose? Why go through all that trouble?" "What's wrong in dating if you're attracted to each other?" First, the purpose would be to get to know each other without the pressure of pleasing each other sexually and without the pressure of making a commitment. Secondly, "Why go through all the trouble of conditioning oneself, disciplining our body and refraining from jumping into a relationship when we are attracted to the person and really like the person?" Because people aren't always as they appear initially. Because a couple months or a year down the road, after you've gotten to know them better, you may no longer be interested in them in a romantic way and if you had resisted the lure for intimacy and developed purely a friendship first, there would be less occasion for heartbreak, fraud and regret.

"What's wrong with dating if you're attracted to each other?"

I believe that godly friendships between a men and women can play important roles in our development and preparedness for marriage. We can learn so much from each other and about ourselves that could help us in understanding our future mates. Actually, such friendships are enriching whether we marry or not. In today's culture, many men and women do not marry until in their 30's and even some in their 40's. You also have those who have divorced or are widowed who may want to remarry. I think that it's important for us to use our season of singleness wisely. If single men primarily socialize with other single men, they won't learn much about women. Likewise, if single women primarily socialize with other single women, they won't learn much about men. If the only time we spend with the opposite sex is when we're dating, then our learning about the opposite sex can be distorted. Physical intimacy and sex can cloud one's judgment and prolong the revelation of the truth of a person's character and compatibility. Then as time progresses, their tendency is to become intimate, then when this occurs, their judgments and decisions may become blurred if they have not made cultivating a friendship important. If instead, you condition your mind to think friendship first when meeting someone from the opposite sex that you find attractive and purpose to pray for them and seek God's will and purpose for them in your life, I believe there would be significantly less broken hearts, fraud and cynicism. Instead, there would be more healthy relationships, more relationships that glorify God and are effective witnesses to the world of God's power and holiness.

Before Raul got engaged, he had dated a few different women and we'd talk about his relationships. I always encouraged him to seek to elevate the woman he was seeing at the given time, and to respect her even if she didn't display respect for herself. We discussed ways in which he could show her respect whether she received it or not. Those were the conversations that inspired the writing of this book. These examples of friendship without the romantic involvement taught me so much and I am so appreciative of these men.

None of these male friends I've been speaking about were homosexual. All were hot-blooded, virile men. Some men don't believe that a normal, hot-blooded man can have a platonic friendship with a woman they find pretty and sexy unless they are gay. These friends of mine, however, very much appreciate and are attracted to the assets of pretty women. They are true, they are godly, and they are respectful, protective, disciplined and honest men. They are wonderful.

These types of friendships with the opposite sex, if done right, prepare us for marriage. Just because a man and woman find each other attractive doesn't mean they have to move into a dating relationship. That may be how it's done in the world, but I don't believe we are to mimic the world's standards for relationships. Rather, Paul says in Romans, "Do not be conformed to the patterns of this world, but be transformed by the renewing of your mind." Too often, however, I don't see a great difference in the way single Christian men and women who are attracted to each other interact. I am not simply referring to sexual involvement, but rather the elementary approach to getting to know each other.

If we keep in mind that in everything we do, in every relationship, we should be seeking to please the Lord, not ourselves, and certainly not the world. Even our friendships will be a cut above. Reflect on some of your past and present friendships with the opposite sex. What would you do differently?

Friendship Training

Application

1) What kind of female friendships do you have?

____

____

2) Do you think that they trust you to protect their purity or have shown them honor based on your relationship with them up until this point?

____

3) How do you define friendship?

____

____

Chapter Eight

Undisciplined

"Brave is the lion tamer, brave is the world subduer,
but braver is the one who has subdued himself."
~ Johann Gottfried Von Herder

"No man is such a conqueror,
as the one that has defeated himself."
~ Henry Ward Beecher

Undisciplined

What is strength? Strength to me is the ability to effectively control one's own mind, body and spirit and make it do your bidding. That's strength. To be disciplined is to be strong. Proverbs 25:28 says that "Like a city whose walls are broken down, is a man who lacks self-control," - vulnerable and weak. The world is full of undisciplined men (and women too). It's sad to say, but so is the church. We who have the Spirit of God fail to actualize the power of the Spirit to control our flesh. We lack the discipline to control our tiredness or laziness and get up to go to church on Sunday and our midweek services. We fail to focus and channel our minds to do those things that we know we should do. If it was, however, a football or basketball game with our friends, or we were called in to work overtime to make some extra money, we can somehow find the energy to get our tired bodies to cooperate, right? Why is that? Why don't we do the same for God? The answer is found in the strength of our desire for that thing or person and the level of mental conditioning. Paul says in Corinthians that we are to "beat our body and make it our slave." He said again in Romans that we are to be transformed by the renewing of the mind, and in Romans that faith (belief and strength) comes through the hearing of the Word.

"Like a city whose walls are broken down, is a man who lacks self-control," - vulnerable and weak.

Physical strength is nothing in comparison to mental and spiritual strength. Take Hitler for example. He wasn't much to admire physically but what mental strength the man had–strength he used to control and destroy millions. In reverse, there are some men who are physically strong, but allow the flesh to rule them, and in some cases destroy them. Look at Samson, he had incredible strength–the strongest man that ever lived and yet a woman destroyed him. Strength is much more than simple physics. The man that can control his mind can control his body and spirit and make a larger and more significant impact than the man that only develops his physical strength.

I met my friend Jason several years ago and he almost destroyed our friendship because of his lack of discipline. He's one of the nicest and funniest guys I know. He's a friend that would go to great lengths to help you out. He loves the Lord and is very outspoken about his faith. However, he had a major weakness. He didn't do a very good job of controlling his sexual desires. One month after we met he tried to seduce me and if I wasn't strong in my walk with Christ, I could have fallen. Obviously, after only one month it's hard to really know someone. I was very perturbed and disappointed. I immediately stopped seeing him on a romantic level. I realized that he lacked self-control and that is always a huge red flag for me. My respect for him diminished. I forgave him but I no longer trusted him.

I learned some valuable lessons from our brief romance. Around the time of the incident that caused me a little grief, we had watched a movie on the television at my place and a particular scene in the show gave me some insight as to why he felt he could do what he did and why many men may feel likewise. The characters in the movie scene were a male detective and a female lawyer. They were working on a case together and became attracted to each other. In one of the final scenes, after the case was solved, the detective paid an unexpected visit to the woman (lawyer's) home. When she opened the door and saw who it was, they chatted for a minute at the door before she decided to invite him in. She got him some coffee and they chatted and reflected on the case. They started to get a bit cozy and next they were kissing. As the kisses deepened, I noticed that the man was more involved in the tryst than the woman was. The man was getting more excited while the woman had started to withdraw. It was obvious to me that she hadn't intended the kiss to go any further and had become very uncomfortable with the situation. The scene ended with her fighting him off and telling him to leave.

At this point Jason makes a very revealing comment. He said, "What did she expect?" She invited him in late at night and allowed him to kiss her." I got the impression that he felt she was, "asking for it." At this point, we had a rigorous discussion. First of all, the character showed up at her door uninvited and even if he was invited in, a cup of coffee and conversation about their case didn't mean that the woman wanted to go to bed with the guy. A kiss doesn't mean she was ready to sleep with him–though that may be what most men may think. Jason didn't see my point of view. I realized that many, if not most, unsaved men would hold to his point of view. Unfortunately, many Christian men would as well, even seasoned ones.

Now regardless of the very different way males and females think and relate, I find Jason's response troubling because in 2 Corinthians 5:17 we are told that if anyone is in Christ he is a new creation, the old is gone and the new has come. We're not to conform to the pattern of this world anymore; we are to be transformed by the renewing of our minds (Romans 12:2). I know we're all a work in progress, I just expected more from him.

Here is an example I can see of a biblical application or conversation that Jason and I could have had and more of what I expected, after viewing the scene above. I expected him to say something more like, "That was a mistake. She never should have allowed him in so late or allowed him to kiss her. He would think she wanted the same thing that he did." Do you see the difference in the approach? In Jason's first and actual response, he sounded in agreement with the guy's response, as though that's what should be expected, which would be reasonable for many unbelievers. In my adaptation, even though Jason understood why the scenario happened as it did, he acknowledged that it was a mistake. He could see it was a misunderstanding of the sexes. It was wrong. When Jason responded the way he did, I didn't get the impression that he saw anything wrong with any part of what transpired.

What I expect from a renewed mind–I'm not speaking of babes in Christ, but one that is being washed and seasoned by the Word of God, is an understanding that as a man of God, you protect, as a man of God, you show honor. What do you derive from God's Word? While yet in sin, Christ died for us…while yet in sin, God loved us and attributed value upon us. You are the head. You are the leader. You are the man. You impute value upon that woman who either isn't showing self-respect or is following the system of this world. As the title of the book I mentioned earlier indicated, we have *A Higher Call.* We are governed by God's standards, not the standards of this world.

Jason and I remained friends over the years and talked about our ensuing relationships with others. I found he had a pattern. He often became sexually involved with the women he dated. He lacked sexual self-control and it led him to make some poor decisions. We talked about it later on because he was going from one relationship to another and went from one relationship into marriage to another and the marriage ended in disaster within a year. A man that cannot control his desire is weak and destined for disaster. Proverbs 25:28 says, "Like a city whose walls are broken down is a man who lacks self-control." In Old Testament times, a city without a wall was weak, susceptible and easy to overcome and so is a man without self-control. He is destined to disaster if he doesn't learn to control himself. One of my favorite passages of scripture is 1 Corinthians 9: 25-27. Apostle Paul was comparing the walk or life of a Christian to that of one training to run in the Olympics.

"Everyone who competes in the games goes into strict training. They do it to get a crown that will not last; but we do it to get a crown that will last forever. Therefore I do not run like a man running aimlessly; I do not fight like a man beating the air. No, I beat my body and make it my slave so that after I have preached to others, I myself will not be disqualified for the prize."

"Everyone who competes in the games goes into strict training. They do it to get a crown that will not last; but we do it to get a crown that will last forever. Therefore I do not run like a man running aimlessly; I do not fight like a man beating the air. No I beat my body and make it my slave so that after I have preached to others, I myself will not be disqualified for the prize."

- 1 Corinthians 9:25-27

The pattern that I observed in him has helped me to quickly identify and avoid others with similar weaknesses. I find that if a man is quick to express his sexual desire within a short period of knowing you, then he's probably in the habit of doing so with other women and therefore, beware. Such a person lacks self-control and is more concerned about his sexual appetite than the lady's well-being. Or he simply fails to think through the pursuit of acting out his fleshly desires and the potential long term consequences and harm. Such a person is led by his emotions and desires, not by wisdom or the Holy Spirit and therefore hurts people and himself. "It is God's will that you should be sanctified: that you should avoid sexual immorality, that each of you should learn to control his own body in a way that is holy and honorable, not in passionate lust like the heathen, who do not know God; and that in this matter no one should wrong his brother or take advantage of him" (1 Thessalonians 4:3-6).

In a similar instance, shortly after I purchased my first home, I found a new church home closer to my new place of residence. My first year at this church, I met a very attractive and very friendly man named Lenny. We spoke a few times and mingled together at our life group. We were both attracted to each other but he didn't approach me directly. One day at a birthday party for one of the ladies at the church, those of us from the same life group were seated at the same table. Lenny went around the table greeting everyone then when he came to me he stood behind my chair and rested his hands on my shoulders and just stood there while he conversed with the lady on my left. He was singling me out and sending a message, at least to me.

Sometime shortly after that day, I got a general email from one of the sisters from the life group. The email was sent out to the members from the life group. Later that day, I got an email from Lenny who must have extracted my email address from the general message sent earlier and that is how it began. We talked a few times and for Christmas that year when he asked what I planned to do. I said volunteer at my neighborhood nursing home. He seemed interested so I invited him to go with me. That was our first "date." A few days later, I don't remember now how it came about, I might have invited him over, I honestly don't remember. That would be kind of odd because I don't normally invite men to my home unless they've been long time friends. At any rate, when I answered the door, Lenny entered and gave me a brief kiss on my lips. This may sound ridiculous to some in this day and age, but I was shocked and immediately on guard. He didn't know me like that. This was only the second time that I'd seen him outside of church. We were not "dating"! Now I should have said something about it but I didn't. I didn't know what to say and often it takes me a while to share what I'm feeling or thinking in such situations. I was trusting because Lenny was endorsed publicly by the church leadership as a great catch. But that small action of a kiss on my lips when he hardly knew me triggered warning bells in my mind and spirit. Soon after Lenny left, I called a close friend of mine and shared my outrage.

What Lenny did signaled an alarm in me. It signaled to me that he was in the habit of doing such things with others on short acquaintance. Which also said to me that if he could do that without knowing me very well, what would he try to do after getting to know me a little better? I was on guard. I didn't immediately stop seeing Lenny and true to my instinct, he did try shortly later to seduce me. When I let him know that I didn't play that way, he backed up initially, but I think he found it hard to believe me and told me so later on. He said that no woman had said no to him before. I couldn't imagine such a thing. No one had said no to him?! Mind you this is a professed "man of God." When Lenny said that, I knew what I was dealing with and realized that he probably preyed on other women in the church.

Now some would say why didn't I cut him off when I realized that? I didn't, but I stopped hanging out with him. I felt as though the Lord put him in my life for a reason and I was going to do my best to be a witness and friend to him. I knew who I was and I wasn't emotionally involved with Lenny. I came to the understanding that here was a man of military rank who was used to being in charge. He'd been on the move frequently, moving from church to church and really had no spiritual accountability in his life.

Within the next month or two, that which I had already discerned became publicly evident. Lenny had apparently been seeing another woman from our church unofficially. For the month of December, she went home to her country for the holidays. It was that Christmas that Lenny and I went out for the first time. Apparently after the young woman returned from her trip abroad and tried to get in contact with him, he refused to take her calls rather than tell her that he was pursuing a relationship with me. But God in his infinite mercy and care exposed him. I befriended the young woman, not knowing she was involved with Lenny. She and I were both from the same country and that common element drew us together.

I invited the young woman over for dinner one evening and was in the middle of preparing the meal when Lenny called and asked what I was doing? I told him that Cheryl was on her way over for dinner and since I was running behind could we talk later? He said, "Cheryl Billings?" I said, "Yes" and hurriedly got off the phone.

When Cheryl arrived, we chatted and had dinner. I was in the early stages of writing this book and excitedly shared a little of the gist of it with her. Somehow we got on the subject of men. (Go figure.) She wanted to know if I was seeing anyone and I said sort of. I remember Cheryl asking if I knew if he had any girlfriends or something to that effect. I said no, because I had specifically asked him when was the last time he'd gone out with anyone and if he was currently involved with anyone. He had told me that the last girlfriend he'd had was three years ago. She asked if I was sure and I told her I was very sure. I felt very confident based on what I perceived to be Lenny's character that he wasn't lying. We talked some more and at the end of the evening, I could tell Cheryl wanted to tell me something but didn't know how or if she should. I remember however, that I said something about how men and women perceive things differently. (I don't know what she said that prompted it.) Sometimes because of how emotional women can be and how relationship focused we are, we can think that because a man is being friendly and spends some time with us, that without a discussion about what's taking place or a discussion of a relationship, that his actions equate to a commitment. I explained, not knowing that Cheryl was involved with Lenny, that some men will take what's being offered them and still not be mentally or emotionally committed to the person.

I knew, even though I wasn't emotionally involved with Lenny, he was also not emotionally involved with anyone either, though he was becoming attached to me. I just knew his heart and mind wasn't anywhere else. So the next day when Cheryl called me at work and told me she believed the man I was seeing whose name I had not revealed was the same man that she had been involved with up until she went away on Christmas vacation, I was a little surprised. She told me that on her way to my house the night before, Lenny called her on her cell and ripped into her and warned her not to try to destroy his "relationship" with me and warned her to keep her mouth shut and leave us alone.

Lenny was out of town that week so when he returned, of course I confronted him with the news. It was as I'd expected. I knew he wasn't in a committed relationship with her, but more so he had started helping her by being there for her in a certain situation. Then as things progressed, he took advantage of the situation. She would go to his apartment to visit and hang out and one thing led to another. But because of her recent divorce and two children, he wasn't interested in a relationship. On the other hand, he didn't mind the companionship and having some fun together. I understand the unregenerate mindset, but it's a sad state of affairs, nonetheless. He expected me to understand and accept it. I understood, but I did not accept it and recommended that he apologize to her as well as confess and repent before God. He refused to apologize to Cheryl. She was very upset because apparently he was very rude to her after he found out she told me the situation. She went to one of the pastors for counseling and they called Lenny in to address the matter. He was unyielding and was therefore asked to step down from ministry.

The whole situation revealed a few things to me. First was of God's love and protection. The Lord had my back. He had revealed to me Lenny's weakness in character early on, so I didn't get emotionally or romantically involved with him. Secondly, the Lord brought it out in the open so that Lenny and Cheryl could grow even though it was a painful experience for them. Thirdly, now others wouldn't be easy prey for him since the church leadership knew his true character and had shut him down.

In both examples, both men showed a lack of sexual discipline and a lack of respect for me. They both professed Christ as Lord of their lives but failed to renew their minds in regards to how they thought of and interacted with women. It's time for a change. This behavior is too prevalent in the body of Christ. Can you help your sister, please?

.

Undisciplined
Application

1) How do you view women?

____

____

2) How would you have treated Cheryl, or a beautiful young lady, if she came on to you?

____

____

3) What is your pattern of behavior in relationships and do you think it pleases God?

____

____

____

Chapter Nine

The Deceptiveness of The Gradual

"All deception in the course of life
is indeed nothing else but a lie reduced to practice,
and falsehood passing from words into things."
~ Robert Southey

The Deceptiveness of The Gradual

Sometimes things just creep up on us. We fall into patterns we didn't intend. We develop habits without realizing it until they're already formed and then they become difficult to break. Those small, everyday decisions that we make can sometimes snowball into a lifestyle we didn't want. So it is with some relationships. When we repeatedly, over time, choose to get involved in ungodly, unhealthy relationships, or simply relationships outside of God's will, we can become deceived or blinded to the truth of our situations.

Just before my 30th birthday, I met TJ. He had a major impact on my life. I met TJ at the skating rink. When I met him he seemed like a black Adonis, tall, broad shouldered, handsome and cut, but a bit lighter in complexion than I liked. TJ was the quiet type, not a man of many words but very sure of himself. The thing I found most attractive about TJ, however, was his faith. He had a great testimony, he was also very family oriented, an outdoorsman, a handyman, owned property, never been married and didn't have children all over the place. (He did have one child.) He sounds like the perfect guy right? So why didn't our relationship work out? Was it me? There wasn't anything "wrong" with him, however, there wasn't anything wrong with me either.

We had some good times, but I was bored. Different things make different people happy. Different things excite different people. I'm not one that lives for the weekends to go catch a movie or go out on a boat or hang out with friends and family. I enjoy all those things but that's not what makes me happy. I loved doing all the things that he enjoyed doing, but not every weekend and all weekend long. I like entertainment, but what makes me happy is ministering to others and making those in need happy. Sharing Christ in real and practical ways is what makes me happy and partnering with someone who enjoys doing that and also knows how to relax and have fun as well would be heaven on earth for me. I knew TJ for 14 years and not once during that time did we do any ministry together. Not once did he recommend it or offer to assist me in any thing I did with the youth nor was he active in any form of ministry at his church. I've always been involved in some form of ministry since I was 15 years old. For many years, I sang in groups and sang solos. I did evangelism, worked in children's church, assisted in the church bookstore and sound booth, ministered through dance and even taught Bible Study. Depending on the need of the particular church that I was a member of at the time, and what the Holy Spirit led me to do, I did. There's always something for everyone to do in service to the Lord and the Body of Christ. So I couldn't fathom, as a Christian, not wanting to do something to help the people of God or to advance the kingdom of God and I certainly wanted to be involved in ministry with the man I married. It took me 14 years to realize and finally accept that TJ wasn't the one for me no matter how nice of a guy he was–our purposes in life were different and we weren't compatible.

What TJ wanted out of life and what I wanted out of life didn't quite blend. He wanted a wife who had a regular 9-5 job, came home and took care of the house and his needs. He wanted the regular weekends off and three weeks a year vacation or more. TJ was content going to work, coming home, running or biking regularly, taking his boat out and hanging with friends and family. That's what most people want and would probably want in a spouse. Now I'm not saying that is not something I would want also, but I'm a driven individual. I'm driven to make a difference in life, driven to achieve and accomplish things in my community, for Christ, and for my family. I've never been content working for any company long term. I've pretty much always had my way on a job. I'm a hard worker and the Lord has blessed me with a sharp mind, a desire for excellence in whatever I do, and a desire to learn and explore. So I usually excel at what I put my hands to do and since I have a healthy sense of my personal worth, I can usually get whatever hours I want. I was employed but had the mindset of a business owner. Since I was a teen I was interested in business and started little entrepreneurial ventures. My parents and two of my brothers are self-employed. So it's in my family's culture.

Business owners tend to have longer, irregular hours in the early years of establishing their businesses. I was in the early years of establishing my business. My hours were long and extended into the weekend. I also had two other business ideas I planned on launching once the first was firmly established. So it was possible that I would be working long hours for some time. I'm highly active and have a big vision. TJ was more laid back and he didn't seem to have much vision. Every time I asked him what his goals were, he didn't seem to have any goals. Now, having said all that, the relationship could probably have still worked if we were both willing to compromise, however, I could not compromise what I felt I was created to do. I could not minimize my vision, but I could compromise my schedule, to some degree. The adjustments would take some time. He would also have to make some allowances and compromises. In the end, I felt trapped and stifled. I didn't have the freedom to dream. I felt hindered, weighed down and concerned that if I married TJ, I would not reach my full potential.

I still seriously considered surrendering my dreams for the stability, loving, caring, protection, patience and sense of family that I knew without a doubt I'd have with TJ. (I suppose that's why it took 14 years for me to let go.) Those are qualities that every woman wants in a husband. (Even as I write this for a minute I ask myself, "Was I crazy for giving him up?") Several years ago, a concerned friend told me the following story of a man that was stuck on a roof top during a flood. He said that the man was praying for the Lord to save him from drowning in the flood. So a man in a boat came by and offered to take him to safety in his boat, but the man declined the offer stating that God would rescue him. Then a bigger boat came by and offered to rescue him and the man declined again, believing God for a miraculous rescue. Finally a helicopter came by to drop a ladder to rescue the man. He declined that, too. The man eventually drowned and when he went to heaven he asked God why he didn't save him from the flood. God said, "I sent three rescue efforts to save you, but you rejected them all." My friend then related the story to me and said, "Beverly, maybe God is sending these different, perfectly fine men to you as possible mates, but you're rejecting God's rescue efforts."

The story sounded good and I recognized it was said to me out of loving concern. However, I would've been suppressing who I am and was created to be by marrying this guy. TJ didn't believe in me or in what I was working to accomplish. I didn't want to be with someone who didn't believe in me. I didn't want to be pressured repeatedly to give up my dreams or to be average. I have to fulfill the purpose for which I was created. If you don't know who you are, who God called you to be and have an inkling of understanding of the work God is doing in you, you will be easily shifted and drawn away from God's plan by circumstances, by loneliness and by your own fleshly desires.

"If you don't know who you are, who God called you to be and have an inkling of understanding of the work God is doing in you, you will be easily shifted and drawn away from God's plan by circumstances, by loneliness and by your own fleshly desires."

I'm thankful for the things TJ taught me both by example and instruction. He taught me about men and relationships. He treated me as though he cherished me the last year of our relationship. He'd finally learned after about 13 years, how to care for me. He really tried and I respect him for it. I gave him a hard way to go, but he wouldn't give up. Instead he would look at me penetratingly and say, "I'm never going to give up on you, Beverly." That was powerful to me. That probably meant more to me than him saying, "I love you." It showed me strength, patience and love. He added value to my life and I hope I did to his. He's a rare one and I hope he finds a good woman.

It was only the Holy Spirit that gave me the strength to do some of the things I was able to do and resist some of the temptations I encountered in our relationship. I see why so many fall and compromise their purity.

I am an affectionate person and so is TJ. It felt like the most natural thing in the world to curl up with him, as a magnet to metal. It never mattered how long we were separated. Sometimes a year or two would go by before we would get back together again but each time we did, it was like picking back up from where we left off, like coming home after a vacation or a business trip and sinking into your favorite chair that conforms to and retains the shape of your body. That's what it felt like when we got back together. My mind and body relaxed and felt comfortable and cared for.

You may wonder how in the world I resisted the draw. How did I resist the comfort and lure of his arms for 14 years?! Saying it wasn't easy is an understatement, but I had set up boundaries in my life to help me. I had made certain decisions in my late teens and early 20's of what activities I would engage in and which I wouldn't, where I would go with a man and where I wouldn't go. I did well when I adhered to those boundaries. I fell when I didn't.

For example, I never took weekend trips or vacations with any of my male friends or boyfriends alone. The one time I did do an overnight trip was with TJ and I did end up compromising my stand. Other boundaries I set up were: I didn't spend the night at their home, nor did they stay overnight at mine, at least not if I was at home, as well. I went to, what some would say, are extremes to avoid temptations.

Several times, I've had male friends come in from out of town and I let them sleep over my house or apartment in the guest room, however, if my mom or family were not there, I let them sleep over but I went over a girl friend's home to stay the night. I know it sounds extreme and ridiculous to some, but the times I failed to do that early on, I almost slept with them. So think what you may. I do whatever I have to in order to honor God with my body. I think of the story of Joseph and Potiphar's wife. She repeatedly enticed him to lay with her and the last time, even tried to trap him into doing so. Instead of succumbing to the temptation which must have been grievous after a while, Joseph ran out on her rather than disgrace the name of God, himself and his master.

Many would not have been strong enough to withstand the temptation day in and day out in such close proximity as Joseph did. Many would have justified themselves as time passed that if they gave into the temptation it would be because Potiphar's wife forced them to or gave them no alternative but to sleep with her. Some would have thought nothing of it after awhile just because that is how sin works. It lures you in sweetly, then binds you with the strength of your own desires and blinds you in its darkness. Remember Samson and Delilah? Only Samson didn't run away from the temptation. He was lured and deceived by Delilah's beauty. She wore down his defenses over time and he finally confided in her the secret of his strength. Delilah shaved Samson's head and had him bound and enslaved. Then they blinded him by digging out his eyes. The lure of sin is most often gradual. Don't be deceived.

"Some would have thought nothing of it after awhile just because that is how sin works. It lures you in sweetly, then binds you with the strength of your own desires and blinds you in its darkness."

TJ had the most opportunity to work on me to get me to compromise my stand against pre-marital sex. For the most part I'd have to say he was a real gentleman. He didn't understand why I went to such lengths in the beginning, nor did he ever come to agree with me. He didn't believe that he would compromise my virginity in the long run; however, purity and virginity are two different things. You can be a virgin and not pure. You can be pure and not a virgin, as well. My goal was to live in purity and remain a virgin until I married. The problem was that it was taking what seemed like a long time for me to accept or do that which I needed to do in order to get married. At first, I just wasn't ready to get married because I was too involved in full time ministry. But the real reason was that there was only one I believed God had already told me was my husband. I just wasn't ready to marry him, nor was I being obedient in praying for him as God had told me to do. In the meantime, I still wanted companionship and found myself getting involved with TJ and others.

I always felt the subtle and other times blatant pressure from TJ in the early days to succumb and stop being "ridiculous." The only problem was that I knew from experience that I wasn't being ridiculous. No matter how much you say, "Oh, nothing will happen," I knew that eventually it would. I'd gone through that test a couple times during my engagement to Kevin and found that it was only a matter of time before the fire will burn you if you keep getting too close. I don't care if you get away with it 200 times. If you give in on the 201st time, it's over. You can't go backwards, or at least it's very difficult to go back. The Lord will forgive you, but your mind and your body remembers and it's hard to fight the demon of lust and desire once you awaken it.

The devil knows this, so he lulls us to sleep saying, "See, nothing happened. It was innocent, you didn't go too far. You didn't compromise your purity." Not this time maybe, or the next or even the next time. The comfort and trust lulls you to sleep, and then the serpent rises up and stings you and takes you out. That's the deceptiveness of the gradual and a killer of the masses.

I once heard a story that if you try to put a frog into a pot of boiling water that it would jump out. If however, you put the frog in a pot of room temperature water on top of the stove, then turn the fire on low and gradually raise the temperature, the frog will allow itself to be boiled. Why? Because the frog will adjust to the heat as the temperature gets gradually hotter; the frog adjusts to the warmer temperature and adjusts his comfort level. The warning signs are there, but all of a sudden when the water gets deadly and starts to boil, by that time it's too late. The frog boils to his death.

The Lord warned me through a message entitled, "The Deceptiveness of the Gradual," preached one Sunday about seven years after meeting TJ. Immediately when I heard the message, TJ came to mind and I became on guard and therefore didn't settle. Even though it took another seven years for me to completely sever the bond for good, I never got completely comfortable mentally or spiritually in our relationship. That is why I broke up with TJ so many times, but I kept going back because of my desire for companionship. The final break up came when I'd convinced myself to accept his offer of marriage. The day that I'd decided to tell TJ I had made up my mind to marry him, however, God intervened and completely blocked me from communicating with him that day. A series of events transpired that left no doubt in my mind that it was not God's will. The following day when I shared with TJ what had transpired, and the conclusion, he still didn't believe and would not let go. He still pursued me for a few more months. I finally had to cut all forms of communication with him so that he and I could both move on.

The hurt was intense the first day we broke up. I cried my eyes out. The second day the pain lessened and I didn't cry. By the third day I was fine. The pain was gone and I didn't miss him. It was incredible. I kept checking myself as the week went on, but I realized that I wasn't in love with him. I had been attached to TJ. It was comfortable being with him on some levels, but once the separation was complete, sad to say, I didn't miss him. It was clear that he was not the one for me. Nevertheless, TJ is a special guy and my prayer and hope is that he will find the woman God has for him.

The wait might seem long, tedious and lonesome, and as a result, it's easy to settle. I spoke with a former co-worker recently. I hadn't seen him in about five years. When I did work with him, we asked him all the time when he was going to get married. He'd been in a relationship with a woman for 14 years back then. He practically put her through undergraduate and graduate school, bought her a car and who knows what else. They didn't live together up until that point and I don't know that they do now. I don't know what his spiritual beliefs are but I don't think they are sexually inactive. When I saw him recently I asked if they were still together. He said yes. I asked if they'd gotten married yet. He said no. It has now been 19 years.

> "The wait might seem long, tedious and lonesome and as a result it's easy to settle."

He's the nicest guy. He's attractive, no vices, doesn't even flirt, works hard and takes care of his dad and his girl. I think he's even putting her through medical school. Now I don't know their personal affairs, but he sure seems like someone who has fallen into the deceptiveness of the gradual as I had. It may seem as though everything is alright and will work out, or so we deceive ourselves and ignore all the signs. Then before you know it, the years have flown by and we've invested so much time and energy, and in his case, money. Some people never wake up out of the deception, may even be quite comfortable in it, but never realize true happiness and their full potential. They settle. Thank God, I woke up.

Are you holding on to a relationship that is comfortable but not God's will for you? You've been in relationship for so long or living together so long and it would be so difficult to break away. But what's God will? Maybe it's a close friendship that you've had since childhood that is holding you back from what you know you should be doing and it's hindering your spiritual progress. How long will you continue in sin and disobedience? The longer you continue in sin and disobedience, the longer it will take for you to wake up and be delivered from that thing and enter into the Promised Land–the abundant life.

The Deceptiveness of The Gradual

Application

1) Is there any pattern in your life that you've "fallen" into or that crept up on you that has you trapped or bound? What is it? It may be an ungodly relationship or an activity that takes time away from church or your family or what God has told you to do.

____

____

2) How did it creep up on you?

____

____

3) What are you going to do about it? (Go to your pastor or a close godly friend and ask for their support through prayer and holding you accountable to change.)

____

____

Chapter Ten

Disbelief, Disobedience and Downfall

"The purpose of problems is to push you toward
obedience to God's laws,
which are exact and cannot be changed.
We have the free will to obey them or disobey them.
Obedience will bring harmony,
disobedience will bring you more problems."
~ Peace Pilgrim Quotes

Disbelief, Disobedience and Downfall

"To him that knoweth to do good, and doeth it not, to him it is sin" (James 4:17 - KJV). How many times have I failed to do what I knew was right? How many times out of fear or disbelief did I disobey God? How many people have I hurt or have suffered because of my disobedience? Remember Jonah? Jonah didn't want to obey God and warn the city of Nineveh of pending punishment for their wickedness. So Jonah ran away. The boat he got into to travel far away from Nineveh and its inhabitants almost perished because of Jonah's disobedience.

The Israelites' story is replete with disobedience. The most memorable to me is their journey in the wilderness. They wandered in the wilderness for 40 years and died in the wilderness because of disobedience and disbelief. They grumbled in disbelief and tens of thousands of them fell. Could our disobedience and disbelief be delaying or blocking the blessings and promises of God? Disbelief is the opposite of faith. Jesus said that he was held back from doing many miracles in those cities where they had little faith. They blocked their own blessings.

As I approached the threshold of 40, God gave me a dream to foretell, forewarn and prepare me of what was to come into my life, and I didn't believe it. As a result I spent the next four years of my life wandering.

The dream was about a man that would take me from one level to another in life. In the dream, this man was showing me through a house that wasn't finished being built. He held my hand as he helped me up the front stairs through the entrance of the house. He held my hand to help me up the stairs to the second level of the house. Then he held my hand again as he helped me up the stairs to the third level of the house, only this time he didn't let my hand go once he helped me up the stairs. He held my hand as he showed me into the master bedroom of the house. I remember clearly looking down at our clasped hands in wonderment. The walls in the master bedroom were unfinished. You could see the wood beams all around. There wasn't any drywall or even insulation in the walls as yet. As we entered the room, the walls started to disintegrate. I saw the fine grainy particles of the wood separating slowly. When we reached the center of the room, he turned me to face him and his head slowly started to bend to kiss me. The walls to the room were now rapidly disintegrating. As his head bent towards mine, I heard the Holy Spirit say, "You can stop this." Then I woke up abruptly.

I was not happy with this dream. In fact I was downright angry. The man in the dream was not the man I was in courtship with. I was not interested in the man in the dream. I was in relationship with TJ and had just been praying for God's will for our relationship and here came this dream about someone else! I didn't want to believe it. I didn't want to listen; I didn't want to heed the warning because it seemed so improbable. However, four months later, TJ and I broke up. Six months after God gave me the warning in the dream, the dream came to pass.

The man in the dream was Sam, my mentor and friend. He became a ploy that Satan tried to use against me to break my stand for purity. Now I don't want this to sound like Sam was brought into my life by Satan for the sole purpose of taking me down. Rather, I feel more like there was a general or specific purpose God had for allowing him in my life and as is the way of our crafty enemy, he saw the opportunity for temptation and sin, and went to work. Satan knows our weak spots and knows how to move in quickly, when we are most vulnerable, and strike and in other cases, simply work persistently to break down our defenses and overcome us when we are weak. He's a master at it. But, greater is He that is in us than he that is in the world, and God in his loving care, will not allow us to be tempted more than we can bear but will make a way of escape for us, (1 Corinthians 10:13).

If you haven't yet faced a similar temptation to get involved with someone you work with closely or minister together with or live close by who you may find attractive and desirable, whether you're married or single, just wait a little while. If you are any threat to the kingdom of darkness, it's coming, and most of the time, it's situations where even if you're single, you know it's not God's will or God's timing. If it was, it wouldn't be a temptation. Temptations come to tempt you to do wrong and sin against God and his will for your life. So for it to be temptation or sin, you have to go against the will of God. It will look good, smell good, sound good, and promise good things. In my case, God gave me a dream to prepare me for what was coming and I still disobeyed! Because I didn't believe when the Lord showed me the unwanted picture in the future, I didn't prepare. My disbelief led to disobedience and a near downfall.

> "Temptations come to tempt you to do wrong and sin against God and his will for your life... It will look good, smell good, sound good, and promise good things."

More than any other man in my adult years, Sam came closest to breaking my stand against fornication. Never before had I allowed myself to be courted by an unbeliever. It snuck up on me. I found myself admiring him and working very closely with him. I admired his faith for he was a man of faith, but not of faith in Christ. I admired his wisdom, his parenting and his leadership, but I knew I could not consider marriage to him. Nevertheless, the close proximity and loving attention he gave me wore down my defenses. Even though God gave me a dream six months prior to forewarn me of what was about to come and told me I could stop it from happening, I didn't heed it. He tried to prepare me for the time of trial and I still fell. I resisted initially because of the dream and because Sam and I were not spiritually compatible but I still don't know how I allowed myself to get involved with him. I think what may have pushed me over the edge into the relationship was that he started attending church with me. That was the ultimate connection. Satan knew how badly I wanted someone that I could worship with and even though the guy was genuine in his initial interest in hearing the Word of God, the primary reason he came was only because of me. After about a month or two he stopped attending.

Interestingly enough, shortly after Sam and I started seeing each other, my pastor preached a message on the kingdom of God and the kingdom of darkness. He did an illustration where he called up two men; one represented the Holy Spirit and the other, the prince of darkness. He stood between the two and illustrated that as we feed on the Word of God and follow the Holy Spirit, we feed our spirit, become spiritually strong and move more towards the things that please the spirit. When we fail to study the Word of God and pray, we are more easily enticed by the devil and drawn away from God and towards that which pleases the flesh. Pastor commented on how attractive the young man was that happened to be representing the devil and stated that the enemy often comes to us looking handsome and appetizing, but beware, it's a trick. (Let me insert a disclaimer here, Pastor was not saying that because a man was handsome or a woman beautiful that they are more likely to be used by the enemy as a ploy to bring the downfall of anyone.)

The lyrics in a popular old song said, "If it feels so right it can't be wrong" is a lie. That's the deception. Just because something feels good doesn't make it right! Or I could use that illustration with drugs, pornography or over eating. In Trinidad, we have this saying, "What's sweet in monkey's mouth is often bitter in his behind." Sin almost always feels good for the moment, but the outcome is destruction–destruction of relationships, of the body, the mind and the spirit.

"If it feels so right it can't be wrong," is a lie. That's the deception. Just because something feels good doesn't make it right!

I remember reflecting on Pastor's illustration later on that day and wondering if Sam could be a ploy of the enemy to destroy me. Ephesians 6:11 says, "Put on the full armor of God so that you can take your stand against the devil's schemes. He schemes and plots ways to cause us to fall. The stronger our stand for righteousness in any area, the more concentrated his offensive onslaught to break us down, especially in that area. He is very crafty but Paul said in 2 Corinthians 2:11 as he was instructing the church at Corinth about correcting a brother that had fallen and grieved the body that they ought now to forgive him,"…in order that Satan might not outwit us. For we are not unaware of his schemes." (Unforgiveness is a powerful tool of

Satan. When we hold on to unforgiveness we think we are hurting others, and we are, but in reality we are hurting ourselves, our children and those we influence by example even more.) We have to be aware of the enemy's plots. In any battle, fight or sport, if you fail to study your opponent or competitor you will fail, for undoubtedly, if they are wise, they have done their homework and have studied you. Make no mistake, Satan knows your weaknesses and sets up opportunities to exploit them. When you study your Bible, you not only learn of the ways of God, though His ways are too high for us to completely understand, but we also become acquainted with the ways of the devil, as well.

In Luke 22:31-32, we find an interesting revelation by Jesus in which he tells Simon Peter, "…Satan has asked to sift you as wheat," and in response Jesus said, "But I have prayed for you, Simon, that your faith may not fail. And when you have turned back, strengthen your brothers." This was right before Peter denied Jesus three times. The Lord warned Peter and still he failed. God went to great care to give me a dream to warn me, and even so, I still failed to listen.

Satan desires to "sift" all of us. It was Peter who turned around and said in his first epistle 1 Peter 5:8 , "Be self-controlled and alert. Your enemy the devil prowls around like a roaring lion looking for someone to devour." Peter had learned his lesson. If we go back to Ephesians 6:12 it says, "For our struggle is not against flesh and blood, but…against the powers of this dark world and against the spiritual forces of evil in the heavenly realms." Satan needs a body to work through and use against us. We must be prepared. Examine yourself, do some soul searching. Identify and acknowledge your weaknesses. Be honest with yourself and allow someone to help keep you accountable. Then prepare spiritual and natural counterattacks.

Here's an example of a counterattack that my former pastor's wife gave me. It may seem minute and even ridiculous to you, but it worked. When I got engaged several years ago, she told me a "secret." She said, "Beverly, to help keep you during your engagement, wear big clothing." She didn't mean unattractive clothing, but to wear clothing a size or two larger so that my attractive figure wouldn't cause me grief during my engagement.

Just prior to her telling me this, I went to visit Kevin, my fiancé, one day and wore a very nice summer dress, no cleavage showing and very little skin showing. However, it was a long knit dress that slightly molded my form. That day I had to fight off his roaming hands. Exasperated, Kevin finally exclaimed, "You don't really expect me to keep my hands off you wearing that dress, do you?" Point taken; I started wearing slightly larger clothing. I think I overdid it occasionally because one day Kevin exclaimed, "Where are you? Your breasts are gone!" I was engaged for one year and though it was a challenge sometimes, I think that slight change reduced our struggle by at least 75%. I was a size five but, when wearing certain materials; I often wore size eight clothing.

That was one of the defensive strategies I employed to help Kevin and I win the fight against fornication during our engagement. Don't get me wrong, I still wore attractive clothing; I just tried to be careful not to wear clothing to excite. When we broke off the engagement, because I didn't compromise my values overall, I didn't have much to regret.

In the case of Sam, however, I did compromise and as a result struggled for three and a half years to overcome the compelling sexual attraction between us. As a result of my romantic involvement with him, I backslid and I feel as though I am still paying the cost of my disobedience, though, thank God I am delivered. I am emotionally free and spiritually restored. If I had to do it all over again, I would never have disobeyed. As Pastor McGraw says frequently, "Sin always takes you further than you wanted to go, costs you more than you wanted to pay and keeps you longer than you wanted to stay."

> "Sin always takes you further than you wanted to go, costs you more than you wanted to pay and keeps you longer than you wanted to stay."
>
> - Pastor Sullivan McGraw

Even though I am no longer bound emotionally by Sam, I still care about him as a friend and a business associate. I now recognize, however, my weakness for companionship. Long periods of isolation are not good for me. I'll do fine for a while, but then I'll seek out or succumb to my desire for companionship with the opposite sex. Unfortunately for me, I find that most men are not just seeking companionship. Either the companionship leads to sexual intimacy or appropriately, leads to a courtship and marriage. Well, both are a problem for me at this time. We know why the first one is out, but courtship and marriage is also out because I'm closed to considering marriage with anyone other than Kevin, at least unless the Lord shows me otherwise.

So I am still vulnerable but knowing one's weaknesses is big part of overcoming the battle. I also have the conviction that I will do whatever I must to guard myself against falling into sin. I don't plan on going out like so many others and Mr. Frog. I'd rather run like Joseph and pay the price of being misunderstood, ridiculed or scorned. I'd rather lose millions of dollars than lose fellowship with my God and Savior Jesus Christ.

This life is so full of distractions, some of which we create ourselves and others the enemy throws in our path to get us off track from God's plan. Some are temptations to draw us away from God and others are tests to strengthen our faith in God. I don't believe in coincidences. Whatever the purpose of Sam's role in my life, I thank God for him and the victory I have through Christ to conquer any temptation and the strength to allow me to be an effective witness. This story could easily have ended otherwise. Even though I failed to take full heed of the dream, it stayed in my mind throughout the time of my involvement with Sam. I'm glad the Lord gave me that dream.

As we journey through life, we have numerous choices and decisions to make every day. Our decisions result in rewards or consequences. Your disobedience or obedience, your belief or disbelief will result in you being lifted up or result in your downfall. As Joshua said to the Israelites so long ago, I believe the Spirit is saying to us today, "Choose you this day whom you will serve." Who will you believe, who will you follow, who will you obey? Who do you want to please?

Disbelief – Disobedience – Downfall
Application

1) Is there something in your life that God has told you to do that you are not doing or haven't done? If so, write it down:______________________________________

____

2) What have been or can be the consequences? What affect has it had or can it have on your loved ones?

____

____

3) What affect can it have on your church family and possibly on your local community?

____

____

4) How do you feel about these consequences?

____

____

5) Now can you envision what God could have done through you if you had obeyed? Write down some of those things.

____

____

6) It's not too late. God can still use you. Repent of your sin. Ask God for direction and step out in faith. He is a merciful God and is faithful and just to forgive you of not just some, but all your sins.

Chapter Eleven

Job (Why Lord?)

"The capacity to be puzzled is the premise of all creation, be it in art or in science" (or otherwise).
~ Erich Fromm

"And yet, this new road will one day be the old road too."
~ Anonymous

Job (Why Lord?)

"Faith is the substance of things hoped for, the evidence of things not seen," and we are instructed to walk by faith and not by sight. Sometimes we just don't know why, but we trust the Lord has a purpose and a plan and we walk in faith believing he will work it out for our good.

Do you ever want to ask God, "Why?" I do frequently, but I'm reminded of Job and Jesus' example. Job didn't know why all the tragedies were coming upon him, but he believed and trusted in God's sovereignty and goodness. Jesus knew why he was suffering and the gravity and brutality of the cross he was about to endure, yet he still pleaded with his Father in the garden of Gethsemane to let this cup pass from him. But thank God he still said, "Nevertheless, not my will, but thy will be done."

> "Nevertheless, not my will, but thy will be done."

As I turned 42, the desire for marriage kicked into high gear. It was constantly on my mind. Late one night in April 2007, I met a pastor in a grocery store who prophesied to me that the next man I would meet would be the one for me and it wouldn't be long now. I was excited and full of anticipation. A couple months later I met three men, two were unsaved and the other was Cedric. I met him during the course of my work.

Cedric is a man that many women would probably love to marry. He seemed like the perfect match for me–he was a business owner and an attorney, intelligent, good looking, fun, and loved the Lord. So what happened? Why didn't I jump at the opportunity to marry him when he asked? Well, there were several reasons. The first stumbling block for me was that he was divorced and I never wanted to marry someone that was divorced. I've heard time and again men (and women) object to my belief and preference to not marry someone who's been divorced. Now if some men don't want to marry women with lots of children, or very heavy women, or women who can't carry a conversation, or women a foot taller than they are, what's wrong with me not wanting to marry a divorcee? I believe that is a desire that God has put in my heart for a particular purpose.

This specific desire began in my early 20's after reading Matthew chapter 19 and Malachi 2:13-16. In Matthew 19:9, Jesus responded to the Pharisees' question about divorce by saying, "I tell you that anyone who divorces his wife, except for marital unfaithfulness, and marries another woman commits adultery." Then in Malachi 2:16, Malachi writes, "I hate divorce," says the Lord God of Israel,…" I believe that what breaks the heart of God, should break my heart too. If the Lord hates divorce, then so should I. I simply didn't want to be a participant. Even in the situations where the divorce was because of unfaithfulness and the spouse had not remarried, I still didn't want to be involved because I felt that God could restore the marriage and I would be getting in the way. If God can heal the sick and raise the dead, surely he can restore marriages, right? So I started praying for marriages, couples that were separated and those divorced but not remarried. It broke my heart when a family member, friend, or even an acquaintance separated or divorced.

A few years, ago after a discussion with my pastor, I went and read Matthew 19 again. Then something stood out to me this time that I hadn't really caught before. In verse 11, Jesus said, "Not everyone can accept this word, but only those to whom it has been given." Then at the end of verse 12 he says, "The one who can accept this should accept it." In other words, some could not, or would not accept this teaching, but on the other hand, some could and those who could – should accept it. I believe I am one who could and should accept it.

God had a specific plan for Hosea. He told Hosea to go and marry a prostitute in imitation of God's relationship with Israel. Hosea obeyed. I'm sure it wasn't an easy thing for Hosea to do. He was probably counseled against marrying Gomer, the prostitute– possibly even ridiculed, like many prophets before him who had radical or unorthodox missions to accomplish for God. Noah is another example. God had a specific plan for him. Through Noah and his sons, God's plan was to rebuild the entire human race. It took Noah well over 100 years to build the ark! (The Biblical scholars differ on exactly how many years, but suffice it to say, it took a long time.) How many times do you think he was ridiculed and mocked during that time? (If you ever have an opportunity to get Bill Cosby's rendition of "Noah and the Ark," get it. It's a great depiction of how incredible an event it was and how ridiculous it must have seemed to the people of Noah's day.)

God's ways are not our ways. His ways and his thoughts are so much higher than our ways and our thoughts. God has a purpose and plan for each of our lives. Some are just more radical than others.

Nevertheless, I tried to bury my uneasiness about Cedric's divorce, but then one red flag after another shot up during our brief romance. It turns out he was a former pastor who'd stepped down from the ministry when he divorced. I never wanted to marry a minister or a public figure because I didn't want to live life under a microscope. Cedric worked almost 24/7. His life was a mystery. I think after his divorce he became a little reclusive. Everything I know about him I know from him. I never met his family, his friends or his partners, nor did he want to meet my friends or family and yet he asked me to marry him about a month and a half after we met! He said I should just trust him.

I had never met anyone like Cedric. He was so used to telling everyone what to do without anyone questioning him and here I was with a lot of questions wanting to get to know this man that said God told him I was his wife. The problem with that was that God hadn't told me that Cedric was to be my husband. I hadn't heard anything though I was praying about it consistently. (Granted, I met him during a time in my spiritual life when I was feeling a bit distant from the Lord. But I knew the Lord was still with me. I'd waited so long for the Lord to send me the right man to marry; I knew he wouldn't let me down.)

Though I really enjoyed being with Cedric, he was a puzzle to me. I loved the fact that he tried to protect me sexually. That doesn't mean that he wasn't still very vocal about his desires. At first his blunt expressions shocked me because he was pretty graphic. But I appreciated his honesty and the way he expressed himself. He was real, he was respectful and he was godly. Kevin is the only other person that bluntly verbalized his desires to me like that, but I was much younger and more naïve back then. I'd never experienced that before and I didn't know what to make of it. So to have Cedric, the minister, do the same, in a natural, respectful way was enlightening and encouraging.

I found Cedric, however, to be a bit temperamental and high-strung. It was his way or the highway. It seemed like every time I disagreed with him or questioned him he'd break up with me and would say things like "this isn't going to work." My take on it was this, if God really said I was your wife you'd work through the disagreements. I was testing him. I wanted to find out who he really was and if he could handle me. I have a strong will and I'm not easily intimidated. However, if you have me in your corner I could be one of your greatest assets. I did not know this man, and yes, I could simply have prayed and trusted his word as that of a minister, but I have a relationship with the Lord too and with a decision so important, I needed to hear from the Lord, as well.

I wanted to marry Cedric. The picture he painted of life with him seemed wonderful. (Now as independent as I am and with the vision I have to do great things, when he said I didn't need to work once we were married, that sounded very attractive to me.) Being with him could possibly have meant giving up my business goals and some of my dreams. I did not see this to be a problem because his vision and dreams were big enough to include me. As long as I felt that I was an active or important part of helping him to accomplish his goals and dreams I thought I could be satisfied. So I was willing to deal with Cedric's high-handed manner. I like a man who knows what he wants, where he's going, has vision and isn't swayed. But he was recruiting me to be his wife, not his employee or a member of his congregation.

Ced had some great qualities about him, but he also had some interesting ways that I just couldn't understand and that bothered me greatly. When we were together there were often times he wouldn't call me for days or weeks while he traveled or if he was upset with me for something I did or didn't do. And soon as he'd dealt with whatever it was, he'd call me and want to pick up where things left off, most times with no explanation. I was expected to understand and not question him. I was doing my best to understand and believe in him and in his proclamation that I was to be his wife but I would have had to turn my brain off and be completely passive. I would've become someone I'm not. It seemed as though I was the only one expected to compromise, however, in a relationship it takes two working together for it work out.

Early one Saturday morning, the Lord woke me up and told me to, "go." That's all he said. He's never done that before. It was about 5:30 a.m. and I don't normally get up on a Saturday until 7 a.m. As I arose, the Holy Spirit told me to hurry. It all seemed very odd. I asked the Holy Spirit if I had time to take a shower and he said "no." So I got dressed and left the house. Now I didn't ask where to go, which Cedric said I should have. I simply dressed, got in my car and headed to his house. I thought maybe the Lord was trying to protect me from something. Maybe a fire or who knows what. (Two years ago I went early one Saturday morning to the office where I worked and the office had been on fire. By the time I got there, the fire was out but the doors were open, confidential files on the floor, etc. I was glad to have arrived there early to take action and protect our clients' information from nosy people in the area.) I didn't know why the Lord was telling me to go and move quickly. I was just so glad to be hearing from him clearly again and didn't care what he wanted me to do, I just wanted to keep hearing his voice and do whatever he wanted me to do.

I arrived at Cedric's home a little before 7 a.m. Now I didn't know what to do once I got there. I'd called him and he hadn't answered. I knocked on the front door and still no answer, so I went around to the back door (kitchen entrance) to knock because I knew it was closer to his bedroom. Still I got no answer so I called again. Finally I heard someone coming upstairs to the kitchen and saw a light go on. I waited and no one came to the door. I thought I'd give him a little time to go to the bathroom or something. I could see through the kitchen blinds that someone of a lighter complexion than Cedric was at the kitchen sink. I knocked again and someone came and peeked through the blinds at the door to see who was there, but said nothing and didn't open the door. The person was a lot shorter than Cedric. I walked away confused and hurt. Because there were two people other than Cedric there, one looked like a young woman and the other a boy (he has a six or seven year old son) and though it was early, Cedric could have came to find out who it was and if something was wrong.

I was quite shook up as I drove to my office, pondering what to do next. Was God trying to show me something? Why didn't Cedric come to the door? Was he cheating on me? Did the Lord want to show me that? Shortly after I got to the office, I received a call from Cedric sounding upset and wanting to know if I was okay. Now this all sounds suspicious, right? I wasn't, however, about to jump to conclusions just yet. I know that Cedric doesn't answer his door to anyone if they come unannounced and certainly not at 7 a.m. I was supposed to be his fiancé, however. What if something was desperately wrong? When I explained the situation he simply asked why I didn't ask God where I was supposed to go. He found it all strange and said God always tells him what's going on. He found it strange that God hadn't spoken to him… Then he said he had two people at the house and that he wanted to take them home first and then I should come by at 10 o'clock for us to talk.

I never asked who was at Cedric's home. I felt he should have told me, now I wish I had asked. When we met at 10 that morning, Cedric didn't explain himself. He questioned my belief that the Lord had told me to go to his house. He once again was about to end our relationship because he questioned my hearing from God. This was just one of the examples of peculiar occurrences during our relationship. There was another time that, on impulse, I decided to drop by (his house and home office wasn't far from my office), not sure if he'd gotten back in town yet and I just wanted to see him. I was going back and forth in my mind whether to drop by since Cedric stated he didn't like unexpected visits. As I pulled onto his street, I noticed his car was there. The passenger door was wide open and I could see Cedric's feet sticking out. I also noticed a woman sitting in the driver's seat. Cedric was reaching for something behind the passenger seat. (I no longer remember if this was during one of the times that we'd broken up or not.) I decided since he had company not to park and instead pulled up alongside the car. He came to the car and I didn't get out. His back blocked my vision of the person in his car. He greeted me, smiled and asked how I was doing? He asked if I'd gotten his text message. I hadn't. That was the extent of the conversation. I said I'd check my messages again and then I left.

I'm not the type of person to fly into a rage and yell accusations. As I left there, I was winded. I thought wow, he's cheating on me. I was dumbstruck and hurt. But, believe it or not, I still wasn't convinced. Some things aren't always as they seem and then again, most times they are. Call me crazy, but I still wanted to give him the benefit of the doubt. I checked my messages when I returned to the office and found a message from Cedric telling me that he missed me. How ironic. If he had truly missed me, he would have greeted me differently when I had dropped by. I got a call a few hours later from him asking me if I was alright. I didn't press the issue, I didn't question him, I just let it be. I thought he would explain to me what was going on later, but until then I was not going to be communicating with him. What excuse could there be for that situation? If it was innocent and Cedric missed me, why didn't he introduce me and greet me properly? I never got a good answer or explanation to how he behaved. Once again, because I wanted to trust Cedric and believe in him as a man of God, I gave him another chance.

Eventually, he and I broke up again and it seemed like every two to three months he would call to see what was going on with me. Confused and lonely, when my ex, TJ called, I agreed to meet him, and somehow I found myself in a courtship with him again. I knew he wanted marriage, but I wasn't over Cedric yet and told him so. That didn't deter him and three months later I had to make a decision of whether I was going to marry him or not. Just as I had convinced myself to say yes, I texted Cedric and asked him what was the last year all about? And as usual he took a couple of days to get back to me. The day I was going to say yes to TJ I got a phone call from Cedric. He began the dialog by saying, "You know you're my wife, you're confused and not hearing from God. You don't need to be in a relationship. You need to spend some time with God and hear from the Lord and stop seeking out men for companionship…"

Cedric proceeded to recount the events of the last year and explain what was going on. I was happy to hear from him, but wasn't too pleased with his tone or some of the things he said. I didn't know if he was really the man for me, but I sure took the intervention as a sign from the Lord not to marry TJ.

Again Cedric disappeared for about two and a half to three months. I got no word from him during that time, so once again I went back to TJ. It was a very confusing time for me. I had two men telling me that I was the woman for them. I very much wanted to get married and have companionship, but the one I believed I truly loved was temperamental and played a disappearing act. The other was there for me, patient and loving but didn't capture my heart or my spirit, but I was tired of being alone. I chose neither. I decided I didn't need to be in a relationship with any man–I needed to focus on drawing closer to the Lord and building my business.

Three months into that commitment, I got another call from Cedric. He was checking in with me to see if I'd gotten married. When he found out I had not, he opened up communication again. By now you may be getting the picture, everything had to be on his terms and in his timing. But I felt I really did love him, which is why I put up with his ways. Needless to say, it didn't work out again. We had another disagreement two months later and he gave up and said he was tired of trying. I finally realized that Cedric just wasn't for me. He wasn't strong enough. God had answered my prayer.

Just before this final break up, Cedric was coming into town (he'd moved to another state) and wanted to see me and take me back with him. I prayed and had my mom and a friend praying with me. I wanted this to be it. I needed to know God's will for me and this man now. I had to make a decision once and for all. Shortly after praying, Kevin came to mind. Every time I would go to say Cedric's name, instead I said Kevin's name. It was a bit aggravating. Thoughts of Kevin started flooding my mind suddenly the week before Cedric's visit. At first I thought that it was just because I was about to make a lifelong decision to marry Cedric and my mind was trying to eliminate the last candidate. However, everything went sour the day Cedric and I were to meet and he abruptly called it quits.

The week before Cedric's visit, I had breakfast with a very close friend with whom I had not spent time with in almost two years. She just happens to be Kevin's sister, Julia. When I shared everything with her, what was coming up, and the decision I had to make, she decided to pray for me. The day of the meeting after Cedric broke up with me for the last time, I called Julia. I told her what had just occurred. She comforted me, then went and got her Bible and read to me the prayer she wrote down and prayed for me the day we met for breakfast. She read, "Lord, show my friend Beverly what's in Cedric's heart. Show her what kind of man he is, in Jesus' name. Amen." The Lord answered her prayer concisely. I was still hurt, but at least I now knew Cedric was not the man God had for me.

I am not angry with Cedric. I thank God for the experience, even though I'm still mystified by it. This is the second time that a Christian man has told me that God told him that I'm his wife and both times they were dead wrong. Both times God did not confirm that fact with me. This last time, however, it seemed almost like the perfect fit. His credibility as a minister of the Gospel, the fact that he's usually right on target about most things in his life, that I fit what he was looking for and that he was the first man I'd met that had almost all the qualities I wanted in a husband made it seem like a perfect match. But God had something else to say about the match. He already had a plan for my life and Cedric wasn't the one for the role of my husband.

I think we often forget God has a plan for our lives and we create plans of our own maybe because of loneliness, sexual desire, pressure from family and friends or, as with many women, we fear that our biological clock might run down and we move out of God's divine will for our lives. I believe, however, that God has specific purposes for each of our lives. As I study the Word of God, I see God's divine plans and purposes exhibited through men and women from Genesis to Revelation. Some of their purposes were grand and we remember their names, like Abraham, Moses, David, Esther, Jeremiah, Jesus and even Judas. Some of their purposes were not as visible or as remarkable and their names may be mentioned briefly or not at all. For example, in Philippians 4:2, 3, Paul says, "I plead with Euodia and I plead with Syntyche to agree with each other in the Lord. Yes, and I ask you, loyal yokefellow, help these women who have contended at my side in the cause of the gospel, along with Clement and the rest of my fellow workers, whose names are in the book of life." Some are just mentioned in general as "fellow workers."

If God knows the tiniest details about us, even down to the number of hairs on our heads (Matthew 10:30), how much more important to him would our marriage be? I think God does have a specific person for us. The question is, do we believe and do we have the faith and patience to wait on God?

Many times we simply won't know what God's plans are. We may not be able to fathom what it is that he's doing through and in our circumstances and relationships. It may take us a while to discern his purpose, but like Job, we just have to trust him, have faith in his love for us, his wisdom and his plan. "For I know the plans I have for you," declares the Lord, "plans to prosper you and not to harm you, plans to give you hope and a future" (Jeremiah 29:11).

My relationship with Cedric was one of the most stressful times in my entire life, yet still I give God thanks. If I had to do it all over again, I would still have chosen to go through it. There was no coincidence in our meeting. I'm bewildered by the experience, but I'm still glad that Cedric's been a part of my life. God used him to show me His love and protection once again. Three times God led me to Cedric's house to reveal to me some inconsistencies and possible infidelity. No matter what it looks like at times in our lives, God is with us, for "…we know that in all things God works for the good of those who love him, who have been called according to his purpose" (Romans 8:28).

Job – Why Lord?
Application

1) What's going on in your life right now that has you stumped as to what God is doing or why you have to go through such a difficult time?

____

____

2) Exam yourself prayerfully and honestly and determine whether your current circumstances are:
    a. Consequences as a result of sin? What was the sin?

    ____

    b. A test to strengthen your faith and build character?

    ____

    c. An attack of the enemy? How?

    ____

    ____

3) What do you know about God that can help you through this trial or attack?

____

____

Chapter Twelve

Good Is The Enemy Of Best

"To obey is better than sacrifice."
~ 1 Samuel 15:22

"'Martha, Martha,' the Lord answered,
'you are worried and upset about many things,
but only one thing is needed.
Mary has chosen what is better…'"
~ Luke 10:41, 42

Good Is The Enemy Of Best

How do you find a mate? How many times did you feel you had found your mate and realized you were wrong? Have you ever wondered, "Is this the one?" Or maybe you were one of those blessed few who met your mate early in life and married her and never doubted that was the one God had for you. For the large majority, however, in Western culture, the first person we dated or courted was not often "the one," your soul mate or the one you married. Recently, the Lord said to me, "Good is the enemy of best" and this time I hope I got the message, though I know I will still be tested on it.

I've met some good guys, even a few great ones and as good as they were they were not the best for me. We have good friends and we have best friends. We have good times and we have great times. We have good jobs and the best jobs. What makes the best, better than the good? It's subjective, isn't it? Because what's great or the best time to you, may not be to me or the next person. What you think may be the best job, may not be the best job for me or the next person.

What about your own good and your own best? For example, on your job, because everyone else does only what is asked of them, you may choose to do the same when you know you are capable of doing much more. You settle for what is norm, for what is average instead of stretching and doing your best. Yet the picture that Jesus gives us is quite different. In Matthew 5:40-41, Jesus says, "And if someone wants to sue you and take your tunic, let him have your cloak as well. If someone forces you to go one mile, go with him two miles." In this passage, Jesus is speaking of how to respond to an evil person, but if we are to treat evil people in this manner, how much more should we do for moral people, family, friends, and the family of God? The Apostle Paul says it another way in Colossians 3:23,

"Whatever you do, work at it with all your heart, as working for the Lord, not for men, since you know that you will receive an inheritance from the Lord as a reward. It is the Lord Christ you are serving."

There is an even higher level of acknowledging good being the enemy of best and that is in reference to sacrifice versus obedience, doing good works versus Spirit-led work, doing good things versus obeying that which God told you to do. God made the difference very clear to me recently and it put so many things into proper perspective. Last year I decided to start roller skating for exercise, for fun and to socialize with some godly people. (I went on the Gospel skate night.) Maybe the second or third time I went, I met a nice, attractive brother in Christ. We had both arrived at the roller skating rink about an hour and a half late. I was running late to meet a girlfriend I'd invited to go skating with me. The brother I met as I arrived that night was tired and had driven, a bit reluctantly, almost an hour to the rink that night. As we entered the rink, I couldn't help commenting on his ragged expression. He shared he had dragged himself there that night.

> "There is an even higher level… sacrifice versus obedience; doing good works versus Spirit-led work; doing good things versus obeying that thing which God told you to do."

We skated together a few times that evening. I introduced him to my friend and at the end of the evening he gave me his phone number to call him. His name was Craig. I gave him a call several days later and we began conversing on a regular basis. Craig was a breath of fresh air, very direct, no flirting and he genuinely loved the Lord.

The evening Craig and I met, my friend Simone and I, who I had invited skating with me that evening, went out to IHOP after skating. We had a great time at IHOP. During our conversation, Simone made an interesting comment that struck me. She said that most of the single men in the church are fake (paraphrase). I think she went so far as to say that she no longer went out with men from the church. She just didn't trust them. I was shocked! Now this young lady is beautiful, intelligent, has a great personality, is ladylike, in her early 30's and loves the Lord.

I've known her for a few years and am familiar with at least one of the young men she dated. So I asked if she found him to be "fake" as well. Yes, she said, he was one of the worst. Now what I gathered to be her definition of "fake," as we talked further, meant to be fraudulent. I didn't get the impression that they were hypocritical, but that in the pursuit of relationships or their conduct within the relationships, they were found to be selfish or impure and left Simone feeling deceived or taken advantage of. I'd heard her say previously that the Christian men still try to "sample the goods," indicating that there was very little difference between their intimate conduct and that of unbelievers.

That is not the first time I've heard such a complaint. I'm thankful that I've met enough of the respectful and honorable kind of men over the years that my experience and encounters with them have positively outweighed my experiences with those who were selfish, seeking self gratification, and unregenerate in their thinking and behavior.

I mentioned that the gentleman I had recently met at the skating rink seemed like an honorable kind of guy and that I'd let her know if my belief turned out to be true after a few months. It was. Craig and I began talking almost every day initially for about an hour to an hour and a half. He was so down to earth, funny, and respectful and knew not only the Word of God, but applied it appropriately. It was fun talking with him. We met only at the skating rink. I wanted to hang out with him and he mentioned it once or twice, but our schedules conflicted. He was a single parent and I think he just wasn't interested enough in me to make that happen. I think it was more my ego than anything else that was peeved that he didn't make more of an effort to hang out with me. But we had the conversation I always try to have with potential male friends early on if we're attracted to each other.

In this case, even though I found Craig very attractive and enjoyed our conversations immensely, I knew it wouldn't go beyond friendship and I like to have a discussion about such things early on. It was about three months prior, shortly after the final episode with Cedric, and right after the six month emotionally purging period. It was a period when I didn't want to be involved in any relationships so that I could really just clear my mind, my heart and my spirit and draw closer to the Lord. In the sixth month, I felt as though the Lord confirmed who my husband really is and as if to say, he hadn't changed his mind from what he told me about so many years before. This time, however, I was in a better place emotionally and spiritually to receive that word. I accepted it and started praying more consistently for the individual. I had peace. No more wondering if the next man that came into my life would be the one. So when Craig came along, I knew his role could be nothing more than that of a friend.

Now just because I knew that, didn't mean that I wouldn't still have to fight the attraction and the ensuing feelings. I think that's where so many of us go wrong. We follow our feelings instead of the Spirit. Thankfully, Craig and I were on the same page. When we talked about where we both were, what our beliefs were about relationships, friendships and God's activity in our lives, we understood each other and agreed not to take things beyond friendship. We were both very open about our enjoyment of each other's company and our attraction, but after we talked about it that one time, there was no need to bring it up again. I still, however, wanted more time spent with him in person, but the Holy Spirit wasn't cooperating and I finally got the message.

"I think that's where so many of us go wrong. We follow our feelings instead of the Spirit."

For example, one Sunday Craig's church was having an evening of dance and ministry. I had work to do, but I sorely wanted to go because I love dance. I'm a dancer and dancers love to go see other dancers but it wouldn't hurt to go and see Craig too, right? The program was from 6:00 p.m. to 9:00 p.m. and I had a lot of work to do, but I told Craig I would try to make it. I was really looking forward to seeing him. Anyway, I didn't complete my work until 8 p.m. and was praying about whether I should still go. I decided to go, but got lost and after 45 minutes of trying to find the street that Craig gave me in his directions, I finally gave up and went home. I was puzzled. Could it be that the Holy Spirit didn't want us to spend more time together, especially alone?

The following weekend as I looked forward to skating again and spending some time with Craig, the Holy Spirit started to work on me. He whispered, "Good is the enemy of best, Beverly." What did that mean in light of the present circumstances, I wondered. What was he referring to? You see, every time I got involved in a relationship I stopped writing. My concentration for everything else went down the drain. I had started writing again on the weekends prior to going skating, but now that I'd started skating and was enjoying myself, I stopped writing. I didn't have the time for both. So that Friday when I really wanted to go skating, I was torn. I felt that I should make the time to complete the writing of this book, but I justified that I needed the exercise and release from a long week and long hours of work. It was also a time of worship, so certainly the Lord would be pleased and my social needs would also be met.

As I went around and around in my head all day as to what I would do that evening, the Holy Spirit's voice insistently grew louder and said, "Good is the enemy of best." But he didn't tell me which to choose. He didn't say, "Don't go skating, stay and write." So I went skating. I had a great time, but the whole time that phrase continued in my spirit. I even shared with Craig the struggle I was having and even though I had a great time skating and great fellowship, I felt like I missed God's best for me that evening.

I have not been skating since that night. Until the Lord releases me to return, I'm doing my best to be obedient. There's nothing wrong with me going skating unless God has told me to do otherwise, and he has. He told me to write. Another reason however I believe he has been keeping me away from the skating rink is because of Craig. That last time I went skating, we skated together a lot and did quite a bit of couple skating which meant there was hand holding or his hand on my waist a good bit of the time. There was definitely some chemistry going on during that time, for me anyway. I think for him also or he wouldn't have slipped and called me babe at one point when I wasn't quite flowing with him. I know God in his infinite wisdom has been deliberately keeping us apart. Why? Because I know I would become emotionally involved or attached to Craig if I spent more time with him even though I shouldn't and either or both of us would get unnecessarily hurt in the end. I might also get sidetracked yet again and who knows what else.

Good is the enemy of best. Sometimes that thing or person that attracts us can actually be quite good, but not necessarily God's will for our lives. Hence, some of the relationships that we get involved in and some of the ventures we pursue. I can't help but think of that saying, "All that glitters is not gold." Just because it sparkles and seems like a good fit doesn't mean we should buy it. Just because he or she looks good or sounds good doesn't mean you ought to pursue or date. What looks and sounds good may not be God's best.

That's why I believe it's so important for us to find out God's purpose for our life. For, as my friend Walter Charles says, "When purpose is not known, misuse is inevitable." If you don't know God's will for your life, other ventures, other people, other's opinions will direct your course and you will still find yourself empty and unfulfilled even though your life is full of things, people and activity.

Rather, there are two verses in scripture that govern my course and these verses I leave with you: "Therefore, I urge you, brothers, in view of God's mercy, to offer your bodies as living sacrifices, holy and pleasing to God–this is your spiritual act of worship. Do not conform any longer to the pattern of this world, but be transformed by the renewing of your mind. Then you will be able to test and approve what God's will is – his good, pleasing and perfect will" (Romans 12:1, 2).

Do you want what's good or do you want God's will? Which is best? The choice is yours. Take time to find God's will for your life in your present circumstances and overall. Everything that has happened thus far in your life, God can use it for his glory. Your life is a living testament. What manner of man will men say you are? More importantly, what manner of man will God say you are? Will you be a vessel of honor, fit for the Master's use? Or will your life be as stubble or hay to be burned and thrown away? Will your life be celebrated?

Choose wisely. My hope is that you will be a man of honor, an example to the men, women and children that are watching you. We need more men to look up to, more men to show us what it means to be a man. We want to celebrate you.

Good, The Enemy of Best
Application

Of that vision, desire or decision you're about to make, honestly ask yourself the following questions below if you want to be in the will of God:

1) The IDEAL Test: Is it in harmony with the Word of God? How?

   ____

2) The INTEGRITY Test: Would I want everyone to know about this decision I'm about to make?

   ____

3) The IMPROVEMENT Test: Will it make me a better person? How?

   ____

4) The INDEPENDENCE Test: Can it become addicting to me? Can it dominate my life?

   ____

5) The INFLUENCE Test: Will anyone be hurt by this decision?

   ____

6) The INVESTMENT Test: Is this the best use of my time and resources? Why?

   ____

** Chapter 12 "Application" questions are adapted from a sermon by Paul Nicholas, Associate Pastor at New Life Worship Center.

Man of God Confession

I am a man whose purpose is to glorify God. Therefore, I choose to manage all my affairs with honesty and integrity. Because honesty and integrity pleases God, and positions me for God's best in my life.

I am a man of vision and faith: Therefore, I boldly pursue God's best without compromise. When the Spirit of God convicts me of my faults and shortcomings, I choose to submit to the Word and overcome every challenge by faith. I live my life so that others may know the faithfulness of my God through my lifestyle.

I choose to act responsibly in all situations.
I owe it to my Lord who saved me;
I owe it to my family who depends on me;
I owe it to my church who instructs me in righteousness;
I owe it to my generation who needs my example;
I owe it to myself, because I am a Man!!!

~ by Melvin Boulware

Recommended Reading

Title	Author
Courage (Winning Life's Tough Battles) -	Edwin Cole
Celebration of Discipline -	Richard Foster
A Turtle on Fencepost -	Allan C. Emery
Maximized Manhood -	Edwin Cole
Sexual Integrity -	Edwin Cole
No More Excuses -	Tony Evans
Fatherhood Principle -	Myles Munroe
What Does it Mean to Be a Man -	Thomas Hart
A Young Man After God's Own Heart –	Jim George
Straight Talk to Men -	Dr. James Dobson
Finding Mr. Right -	D. Nile River
A Higher Call -	Harold Bell Wright
Shepherd of the Hills -	Harold Bell Wright

www.ingramcontent.com/pod-product-compliance
Lightning Source LLC
Chambersburg PA
CBHW072143280526
45788CB00002B/756

* 9 7 8 1 4 5 3 8 5 7 9 0 8 *